RECIPES FROM CAMP TRILLIUM

RECIPES
FROM
CAMP TRILLIUM

LOUISE
GAYLORD

LITTLE
MOOSE
PRESS®

Beverly Hills, CA

Little Moose Press
269 S. Beverly Drive #1065
Beverly Hills, CA 90212
Tel: 310-862-2574 • Fax: 310-564-1991
www.littlemoosepress.com

Publisher's Cataloguing-in-Publication

Gaylord, Louise.
    Recipes from Camp Trillium / Louise Gaylord. -- 1st ed. --
BeverlyHills, Calif. : Little Moose Press, c2009.

        p. ; cm.
        ISBN: 978-0-9786049-6-7
        Includes index.

        1. Cookery, American. 2. Dinners and dining.
    3. Home economics. I. Title.

TX715 .G39 2009   2009937323
641.5/973--dc22   0911

Printed in the United States of America

Cover photo: Will Macfadyen
Book Consultant: Ellen Reid
Book and Cover Design: Bacall:Creative
Editor: Pamela Guerrieri
Indexer: indexer@lightspeed.net

For childhood's opening bloom,
For sporting youth to stray in,
For manhood to enjoy his strength,
For age to wear away in.

—from "Yarrow Visited"
by W. Wordsworth
September 1814

PREFACE

Our family is the fifth family to own Camp Trillium, often referred to as "Camp Thrill-em" on beautiful summer days when sunlit diamonds sparkle atop the lake water, or "Camp Trillion" when payments for the camp's multitudinous pleasures are exacted.

My first experience in the Adirondack woods goes as far back as early October, 1962, when my husband's brother invited us to join his family for a few days at an outlying camp.

Having never experienced such an outing and since it was October, my Texan mind thought "cold," so I packed accordingly. What a joke! The temperature was in the high 80s. My woolens never made it out of the suitcase. Instead, I found myself in borrowed khakis and cotton tops, crammed into the third seat of a station wagon along with several nephews and nieces as the group set out along narrow, bumpy roads winding through depressingly barren forests. An early and unexpected windstorm had blown away the highly-touted and much-anticipated fall foliage.

The far distant Proctor Camp meant "roughing it" in the truest sense. No electricity, no running water, no indoor plumbing. Once darkness fell and the Colman lamps were doused, the silence of the night mingled with sounds of porcupines gnawing on the foundation and field mice scrambling back and forth across the worn wooden floors—no small comfort for a tenderfoot like me.

After three long, long days in the wilderness, we returned to civilization and the Cuban Crisis, which seemed an eerie contrast to all we had experienced. That was when I added the Adirondacks to my short list of never-ever-do-that-again.

But as fate would have it, we were invited for a second visit in 1965 and then a third in 1968. Fortunately, Camp Proctor had been swept from the agenda to be replaced by a rambling, comfortable camp at the edge of a beautiful lake. After spending the better part of July in that camp where we entertained friends from Houston, we signed on.

In 1969, we rented a cottage and enjoyed exploring the Preserve on our own. The days flew by and once again we sadly left our mountain greenery retreat for the sauna-like city of Houston.

In early 1970, we heard that Camp Trillium was available to rent during the coming summer. Though we had been to cocktails at the boathouse and I had fallen in love with the camp, I suffered mixed emotions. Camp Trillium seemed a long way down the lake from the daily excitement of the cottages, but certainly not as far away from civilization as Proctor.

After much deliberation, we decided to take the leap. It was the best decision we ever made. For the last forty summers our family has spent strings of wonderful days enjoying the special beauty of the Adirondack woods. And each summer we appreciate it just as much as the last.

A BRIEF HISTORY OF CAMP TRILLIUM

Lot 18, the original site of Camp Trillium, was purchased in 1900 by John A. Chambers of Morristown, New Jersey, who five years later in 1905 purchased Lot 19. The camp, then known as the Chambers Camp, was enjoyed by the owner until his death in 1908 and remained in his estate until 1910.

In the spring of 1910, Dr. Hermann Michael Biggs, General Medical Officer of the City of New York Department of Health and Scientific Director of the Rockefeller Institute, and his wife visited the Chambers Camp. And, as noted in Dr. Biggs' biography, "He gathered a bouquet of trilliums under the spruce woods and gave them to Mrs. Biggs who said, 'If we buy this place, we will name it Camp Trillium.'"

As further quoted in his biography, *The Life of Hermann M. Biggs*, by C.E.A. Winslow, published by Lea & Febiger in Philadelphia, 1929, pg. 22 chronicles his growing adoration for the Adirondacks:

Here, for the rest of Dr. Biggs' life, he found inexpressible rest and refreshment. Leaving the sleeping car at Thendara, driving four miles to the clubhouse on Little Moose and then crossing the lake by the efficient Adirondack Guide boat, the responsibilities for the tuberculosis-ridden tenements of New York City dropped from his shoulders. Camp Trillium, with the lake on one side and the wooded hills behind, was the real home to which he looked with longing through the winter. Here with Lamont the guide, he planned for the enlargement and improvement of the camp, clipped the hedges and planted the garden, and in the evening watched the sun set over the lake or walked over the trails to catch a glimpse of the flash of white from the tail of a deer plunging off through the undergrowth.

After the doctor's death in 1920, Camp Trillium remained in the Biggs family until 1933, when the property was sold to Harry Parker and his wife Edythe of New York City. The Parkers had no children, but from the looks of old photographs, they had a grand time entertaining guests and enjoying fishing expeditions around the Preserve.

On a sad note, when the original two-story boathouse burned to the ground circa 1945, a large formal dining room and several bedrooms were lost forever. It is said that the Parkers' maid had left on an iron. There are several snapshots of the maid sitting dejectedly in the ruins of the boathouse. Dates are not available on the rebuilding of a second boathouse, which became a "party house" with a small kitchen and bar. Unfortunately, no bathroom was added and to this day there are trips into the woods to "kill a fern."

Lot 16 was finally acquired by the Parkers in 1953 from the estate of Joanna W. Shepard Bright, daughter of Augustus D. Shepard, principal architect of many Adirondack structures including Camp Trillium.

In 1965, Lots 16, 17, 18, and 19 were purchased from the widow of Harry Parker by Dorothy and Radcliffe L. Romeyn, who were then living in Venezuela. Mr. Romeyn had been coming to the Adirondacks since his early childhood. His parents and the Alfred Schoellkopfs of Buffalo were close friends and in 1922 they jointly built Camp Cedarbank.

Nearly two decades passed, and in 1981 one-half of Lot 17 and all of Lots 18 and 19 were purchased from the Romeyns by Ted and Louise Gaylord of Houston, Texas, who had rented the camp from the Romeyns from 1970 until its purchase.

One wonderful plus comes with the purchase of a camp, at least in the case of Camp Trillium. With the exception of personal belongings, the buyer gets the camp complete with existing furniture, china, silver, linens, and other accessories.

During our explorations of the camp we discovered several rare pieces of Stickley furniture, a wonderful crank-up record player stashed in one of the lower cupboards of the dining room, and upstairs built-in drawers filled with lovely sleigh blankets, linen hand towels, and cocktail napkins. Since the servants, along with a lot of personal wealth, had disappeared in the Great Depression, the linens were carefully returned to the drawers where they remain today.

As of this printing, Camp Trillium remains in the Gaylord family and our hope is that it will continue to be so for many years to come.

ABOUT THE TRILLIUM

(Condensed from an article on www.easywildflowers.com)

The trillium, Latin *tres* for three and *lilium* for lily, is a charming native woodland wildflower found growing in shaded areas over most of the Eastern United States. The plants demonstrate a simplistic elegance in three whorled leaves and a large three-petaled white flower with slightly ruffled edges. They grow from an underground rhizome that "travels" beneath the topsoil.

The delightfully unusual white flowers of wild trillium, which are sensitive to light, are a harbinger of spring, growing wild in moist areas beneath deciduous trees or very tall conifers. Trilliums bloom for two to three weeks in April and May and often fade to pink as they age, finally going dormant with the heat of summer.

Trillium plants can live for twenty-five years or longer and usually do not flower until they are several years old. Populations of white trilliums expand slowly and may be jeopardized in areas where they are heavily browsed by deer because the plants will die out after several years of repeated browsing.

Picking a trillium flower does not necessarily kill the plant, but damage will result if the green leaves are removed as well. The leaves are needed for photosynthesis and if picked will not re-grow until the following year. Even then, the re-growth may not occur since it depends on the size and maturity of the rhizome beneath the plant.

INTO THE WOODS FOR AN OUTLYING CAMP COOK-OUT

Though our generation has given up spending overnights in outlying camps, the family still enjoys lunch or dinner in the rustic beauty of the woods. As one can see from the list below, dining in the woods takes quite a bit of preparation.

While the majority of the group will hike into the designated picnic area, others will drive the food and drink to the spot, and by the time the hikers arrive, the fire is started and the rest of the spread is laid out.

One of the unique features of the Adirondacks is the versatile Adirondack Pack Basket (www.adirondackpackbaskets.com) woven from a heavy gauge reed for sturdiness. The rim has a handle grip formed into the back of the basket. Each basket has a wooden base inside and pressure treated runners on the outside to protect the bottom of the basket. A harness or shoulder strap is attached to the basket by ears inserted at the base.

Depending on the size of the group, any number of pack baskets may be employed. After the food and supplies are unloaded from the basket, it can be lined with a trash bag and serve as a convenient trash repository, or fill it with ice to cool down drinks.

LIST FOR COOK-OUT

2 large adirondack pack baskets
2 coolers
Hot dog & hamburger grills

Cooler One: Iced

Wine
Fruit juices
Beer
Soft drinks
Water

Cooler Two: Iced

Pre-formed hamburgers
Hot dogs
American cheese squares: white &
yellow

Condiments:

French's® yellow mustard
Dijon
Mayonnaise
Catsup
Dijonaise®
Pickle relish
Sliced and diced onions
Iceberg lettuce
Pickles: butter, dill, & sweet
Sliced tomatoes
If available: potato salad & coleslaw

Pack Basket One:

Graham crackers
Hershey® bars
Marshmallows
Hamburger & hotdog buns
Chips

Pack Basket Two:

Spatula
Long fork
Knife
Scissors
Wine opener & beer opener
Matches & fire-starter
Fire gloves,
Paper plates
Napkins
Plastic cups
Trash bags (for garbage and
recycling)
Paper towels
Pam® out door grill spray
Insect repellent
Handi-wipes®

WITH GRATEFUL THANKS TO THOSE WHO CONTRIBUTED RECIPES

Through the past forty summers we have been lucky to boast several honest-to-goodness chefs in the family, as well as many accomplished cooks. And we feel extremely fortunate to have had a steady stream of guests visit Camp Trillium who offered to step into the kitchen and create a wonderful dinner for the rest of us.

Listed below are the contributors who were kind enough to share their recipes. Further thanks to those unsung heroines who cooked and didn't document their recipes.

Virginia Abercrombie, "Aunt Cas" Castelle Boller, "Nanny" Florence Brogniez, Corrine Buchanan, Patsy Burk, Lucy Burnap, Jack Campbell, Julie Chamberlain, Peggy Clute, Barbara Collum, Evelyn Gwaltney Colson, Peggy Crowe, Jan Davis, Dick Delmarle, "Nana" Marion Gaylord Delmarle, Rosetta De Vito, "MM" Mary Merrill Ewing, Eric Fairchild, Kathy Farrell, Dianne Foutch, Mary Kay Gaedcke, Bud Gaylord, Claire Gaylord, Jackie Gaylord, Melanie L. Gaylord, Ritter Gaylord, Ted A. Gaylord, Ted Gaylord, Vickie Gaylord, Paul Gilette, Jayne Gilligan, David Gonzales, Mickey Hargrave, Kelly Higgason, Guida Jackson Laufer Hume, Ida Luttrell, Missy Macfadyen, Jennifer Macfadyen, Geri Noel, Isabel Oppen, Jackie Pelham, Nicole Peterson, Nancy Power, "Granma" Betsy Robertson, Carol Robertson, Masey Robertson, Anne Robertson Seay, Andrea & Pete Sitterle, Suzy Swanson, Connie Tierney, Mary Faye Way, Mark Webster, M.D., and Audrey Wolcott.

—Louise Gaylord

TABLE OF CONTENTS

Nota Bene: EVOO Stands For Extra Virgin Olive Oil

BREAKFAST & BRUNCH

EGGS IN GENERAL

EGGS (continued)

HORS D'OEUVRES & NUTS

HORS D'OEUVRES & NUTS (continued)

DIPS, MARINADES, DRESSINGS & SAUCES

DIPS, MARINADES, DRESSINGS & SAUCES (continued)

SALADS

SALADS (continued)

SOUPS

SOUPS (continued)

SIDE DISHES

SIDE DISHES (continued)

SIDE DISHES (continued)

ENTREES

ENTREES (continued)

ENTREES (continued)

MICROWAVE HINTS

AFTERS

AFTERS (continued)

COCKTAILS

COCKTAILS (continued)

TRILLIUM TIPS

BREAKFAST
& BRUNCH

NANA'S FOOLPROOF POPOVERS FOR 8

1 cup all-purpose flour
¼ tsp. salt
2 large or 3 small eggs
1 cup milk
1 Tbsp. melted butter

Note: All ingredients should be at
room temperature.

Preheat oven to 450 degrees. Butter
8-10 custard cups and place on a cookie
sheet. If using Teflon cupcake pan,
do not butter the pan. Sift flour, then
add salt. Beat eggs in a separate bowl
until frothy, then add 7/8 cup milk and

butter. Stir the liquid slowly into the sifted ingredients. Beat the ingredients until they
are well-blended.

Pour the batter into the cupcake pan ¾ of the way full.

Bake for 40 minutes.

Poke with a toothpick to let out steam. Remove from cups immediately.

POPOVERS FOR 10

2 cups all-purpose flour
1 tsp. salt
6 small eggs
2 cups milk
6 Tbsp. butter

Preheat oven to 375 degrees. Beat eggs lightly. Add milk and melted butter, then stir to combine. Gradually stir in sifted flour and salt. Beat until mixture is smooth. Do not overbeat. Strain if still lumpy. Pour mixture into pitcher, then fill cups ¾ of the way full.

Bake at 450 for 50 minutes. Remove popovers from oven, cut several slits in the top, and return to the oven for 5–10 minutes. Immediately remove popovers from pan and serve warm.

YORKSHIRE PUDDING FOR 6

7/8 cup all-purpose flour
½ tsp. salt
½ cup milk
2 eggs
½ cup water
Beef drippings

Note: All ingredients must be at room temperature.

Preheat oven to 400 degrees. Sift flour into a bowl and add salt. Press hole in the center and pour milk in center. Stir. Beat in eggs until fluffy. Continue to beat batter. Add water, beating batter until large bubbles rise. Let stand covered and refrigerate for 1 hour, then beat it again. Have a 9x12 heated oven-proof dish ready containing ¼ inch of hot beef drippings. Pour batter over drippings; it should be 5/8 inch high.

Bake 20 minutes. Reduce heat to 350 and bake for 10-15 minutes longer. Serve hot.

NANA'S SAUTÉED BREAKFAST TOMATOES

1 tomato
Basil
Sugar
Salt
Pepper
Butter
Toast/English muffin

Slice one medium fresh tomato. Sprinkle with basil leaves, sugar, salt, and pepper to taste. Sauté on each side in butter. Serve on toast or English muffin.

SOUR CREAM SOUFFLÉ FOR 8

½ cup freshly grated Parmesan
1 ½ cup sour cream
½ cup sifted flour
5 egg yolks
1 tsp. salt
¼ tsp. cayenne
2 tsp. chopped chives
7 egg whites

Preheat oven to 350 degrees.

Butter a 2-quart soufflé dish. Coat with some of the cheese and refrigerate. Whisk sour cream and flour together. Stirring briskly, add yolks one at a time. Stir in the rest of the ingredients.

Beat egg whites until firm. Fold into mix with rubber spatula.

Bake 30-35 minutes.

CRABMEAT DELIGHT FOR 12

1 small can fancy shredded crabmeat
1 stick butter, melted
1 jar Old English® cheese spread
1 ½ Tbsp. mayo
3 tsp. garlic grated
6 English muffins, split

Mix butter, cheese spread, mayo, and garlic. Add shredded crab. Spread on muffins and freeze for 10 minutes. Broil until bubbly.

CRAB ON ENGLISH MUFFINS FOR 4

2 English muffins
1 can fresh lump crabmeat
Green onions
Lemon juice
1 tsp. mayo
2 3-oz. packages cream cheese
2 egg yolks
1 minced onion
2 Tbsp. Nance's Sharp & Creamy Mustard®

Butter and toast two English muffins. Mix crabmeat, chopped green onions, lemon juice to taste, and mayo. Spread mixture on halves.

Mix cream cheese, egg yolks, minced onion, and mustard. Add mixture on top of English muffins.

Brown under broiler.

GARLIC CHEESE GRITS

6 cups water
2 tsp. salt
1 ½ cups uncooked grits
1 stick butter
3 eggs, well-beaten
1 lb. (4 cups) sharp cheddar, grated
1–3 garlic cloves, minced
Cayenne pepper to taste

Preheat oven to 350 degrees.

Bring water and salt to a rapid boil. Gradually stir in grits. Cook until water is absorbed.

Stir in butter bit by bit. Gradually add eggs, cheese, garlic, and cayenne pepper. Pour into a greased 2 ½ qt. casserole. Top with additional cheese and cayenne for color.

Bake for 1 hour and 20 minutes.

CORRINE'S MUSHROOMS & WINE ON ENGLISH MUFFINS

Recipe feeds 8.

½ cup melted butter
¼ cup grated onion and juice
2 lbs. sliced mushrooms
1 ¼ tsp. salt
White pepper
¼ tsp. nutmeg
½ cup sour cream
½ cup heavy cream
English muffins

Melt butter. Add onion and cook over low heat for 3 minutes. Add mushrooms and seasonings. Cook until browned and remove from heat. Add sour cream and heavy cream. Heat, but don't boil. Serve on toasted English muffin halves.

BASIC CRÊPES

Recipe makes 20–24 crêpes.

1 cup flour
2 Tbsp. sifted flour
1 pinch salt
1 ½ cups skim milk
1 Tbsp. melted butter
1 ½ Tbsp. brandy
3 eggs, well-beaten

Combine flour, salt, milk, butter, brandy. Add eggs. Beat until smooth. Cover and let stand 1 hour.

*For sweet crêpes add ¼ cup powdered sugar and substitute Cointreau for brandy.

NOTES AND VARIATIONS

EGGS IN GENERAL: CASSEROLES, STRATA, FRITATA, DEVILED, & OTHER

BEST WAY TO HARD-BOIL EGGS

To determine whether an egg is fresh, immerse it in a pan of cool, salted water. If it sinks, it's fresh. If it floats, toss it.

Nota bene: To perfectly center the yolks, before cooking wrap a rubber band around the egg carton and refrigerate the carton on its side for several hours or overnight.

Place as many eggs as needed in a single layer in a saucepan. Cover them with an inch of cold water and a pinch of salt to prevent them from cracking. Bring the water just to a boil. Turn off heat and cover the pan let eggs sit for 10 minutes in hot water. Use a slotted spoon to transfer them to a bowl of ice water to cool. This method produces a moist yolk.

OR

Place eggs in pan large enough to hold them in a single layer and cover with cold water. Bring to a boil, cover, turn off heat, and let eggs sit 15 minutes. Drain and run under cold water until eggs are completely cooled.

OR

For a firmer yolk, remove the pan, pour off the water, and let eggs cool naturally. Or remove the pan from the heat, cover, and let stand 20 minutes.

OR

TRY STARTING EGGS IN BOILING WATER. GUARANTEED NOT TO STICK TO SHELL. The cooked eggs may be stored in the shell up to three weeks or peeled immediately.

To peel cleanly: Tap egg gently all around on a hard surface, then roll lightly under your hand until the shells crush into a network of tiny pieces.

Begin peeling from the broad end. You should get a perfectly peeled egg.

HOW TO WHIP EGG WHITES

1. Be sure the whisk and bowl are free of all traces of fat (that includes egg yolk).

2. Place a towel under the bowl so it won't slip.

3. Start with room temperature eggs for best results.

4. Beat until a droopy peak forms. If you want to add cream of tartar to stiffen, or add sugar for meringues, do it now.

5. Continue until the peaks are at maximum volume and the surface remains moist and glossy.

6. Don't over-beat. Once the egg whites lose their moisture, they deflate.

NANA'S EGG CASSEROLE

1 small loaf bread, crusts off, torn into 1" squares
14 oz. medium cheddar cheese
5 eggs, beaten
3 cups milk
5 eggs, beaten
1 tsp. dry mustard
¼ lb. butter
1 cup sliced mushrooms

Line casserole dish with 1/3 of bread squares. Add layer of ½ cheese, then a layer of 1/3 of bread. Add remaining cheese and remaining bread on top. Mix milk, eggs, and dry mustard; pour over the layers.

Cover and refrigerate overnight.

Melt butter, brush top of bread layer. Cover with sliced mushrooms, brush with butter.

Bake at 350 degrees for 1 hour, checking after 45 minutes.

JAYNE'S STRATA WITH SPINACH

Recipe feeds 8–10.

   1 large onion, chopped
   3 peppers, chopped
   2 Tbsp. EVOO
   4–5 croissants or brioche, torn
   2 bunches spinach, stemmed and strewn
   8 eggs
   1 qt. milk
   ½ lb. cooked bacon strips, crumbled
   1 lb. cheddar, cut into chunks (½ white cheddar, ½ yellow cheddar)
   2 cups Parmesan cheese

Preheat oven to 350 degrees.

Sauté onions and peppers in EVOO. Set aside. Layer half the croissants/brioches on bottom of baking dish.

Blend eggs and milk. Pour ½ mixture over dough. Add remaining bread on top, then add onions, peppers, and crumbled bacon.

Bake for 20 minutes, then sprinkle on 1 cup Parmesan cheese. Wait a few minutes; sprinkle on remaining 1 cup of Parmesan cheese.

Note: This recipe can include almost anything you have in the fridge.

BAKED RED PEPPER FRITTATA FOR 4

2 red bell peppers
2 onions, thinly sliced
3 Tbsp. EVOO
6–8 eggs
2 Tbsp. cilantro
2 Tbsp. basil leaves
Salt and freshly ground pepper to taste
Butter
6 Tbsp. breadcrumbs, divided
½ cup grated Fontina cheese

Preheat oven to 375 degrees.

Core, seed, and julienne peppers. In a medium sauté pan, sauté peppers and onions in olive oil until soft and lightly golden. Let cool.

Crack eggs into separate bowl and beat lightly with a fork. Add the onion/pepper mix, then the herbs and salt and pepper.

Butter a 10-inch baking dish and sprinkle on 4 Tbsp. of the breadcrumbs. Pour in egg mix; sprinkle with cheese. Cover with remaining breadcrumbs.

Bake for 20 minutes or until the frittata is slightly puffy and firm. Serve hot, warm, or cold.

PATSY BURK'S BREAKFAST CASSEROLE FOR 10

    1 regular pkg. Owens ground sausage
    1 dozen eggs
    1 box Pepperidge Farm seasoned croutons
    1 tsp. salt
    ¼ tsp. dry mustard
    1 cup milk
    2 cups shredded cheddar cheese

Sauté sausage and drain. Beat eggs. Combine all ingredients except for 1 cup cheddar. Stir in thoroughly. Pour into casserole dish. Top with remaining cheddar.

This must sit in the refrigerator overnight before baking.

Bake at 350 for 30–40 minutes.

EGG CASSEROLE FOR 6

    7 slices white bread, crusts removed
    Butter
    1 lb. ground sausage
    4 cups shredded cheddar cheese
    6 eggs
    1 tsp. salt
    1 tsp. dry mustard
    2 cups half & half or milk

Lightly butter each slice of bread and place in a 9x13" buttered glass baking dish. Brown sausage. Drain and pat with paper towels. Sprinkle sausage and cheese over bread.

Beat eggs. Add salt, dry mustard, and half & half (or milk). Beat mixture again. Pour egg mixture over bread, sausage, and cheese.

Cover and refrigerate overnight. Bake uncovered at 350 for 45 minutes or until the casserole is bubbly and lightly brown on top.

MISSY'S MICROWAVE EGG

1 Tbsp. margarine
1 egg
½ cup milk

In a small glass bowl, melt margarine. Add egg and milk and beat. Microwave on medium-high heat for one minute, watching carefully as it cooks. Add onions, ham, or a variation of extras to make an omelet.

DIANNE FOUTCH'S MICROWAVE EGG

1 egg
1 paper towel

In a small glass bowl, break egg. Cover with paper towel, being sure ends are well tucked in under bowl. Microwave for 28 seconds or less.

OMELETS TO ORDER FOR A LARGE CROWD

Plan on two eggs per person.
Note: It is easier to mix all the eggs and any seasonings in a large bowl in advance.

Put out a variety of ingredients: shredded cheese, chopped cooked ham, chopped sautéed onion, sliced mushrooms, chopped red and green peppers—all slightly cooked or microwaved.

Have each guest write his or her name on a quart-sized freezer Ziploc® bag with a permanent marker. Add two ladles of egg and any ingredient they want. Shake it up and make sure to get the air out of the bag before you seal it.

Place 6–8 bags into a large pot of rolling boiling water for 13–15 minutes— 13 minutes for fewer ingredients, 15 minutes for more.

Open the bag and the omelet will easily roll out. Serve with English muffins, toast, or fresh fruit.

DEVILED EGG RECIPES

GUIDA'S DEVILED EGGS

12 peeled hardboiled eggs, halved lengthwise
1 tsp. white vinegar
1 tsp. white wine
1 Tbsp. Dijon mustard
1 Tbsp. mayo
¼ cup onion shavings
Pepper

Place yolks in a bowl and slightly moisten with white vinegar and white wine. Mash until thickly mushy; add Dijon mustard and mayonnaise, along with thin shavings from a juicy onion. Add pepper. Taste to be sure the mixture is slightly vinegary.

Heap mixture into egg white halves and sprinkle with paprika. Garnish with capers, salmon roe, or whatever else happens to be lying around.

GOOD DEVILED EGGS

8 shelled hardboiled eggs, halved lengthwise
½ cup plain fat-free yogurt
2 Tbsp. low-fat mayo
1 tsp. curry powder
½ tsp. salt
½ tsp. grated peeled fresh ginger
1/8 tsp. hot pepper sauce
2 Tbsp. chopped green onions (optional for garnish)

Combine egg yolks with remaining ingredients. Beat with mixer until smooth. Spoon 1 Tbsp. mixture into each egg-white half. Cover and chill.
Note: 34 calories for each half.

DIJON DEVILED EGGS

12 peeled medium hardboiled eggs
¼ cup mayonnaise
¼ cup Dijon mustard
4 Tbsp. butter at room temperature
1 tsp.fresh lemon juice
¼ tsp. cayenne pepper
Salt
Freshly ground white pepper

Peel eggs and cut in half lengthwise. Remove yolks and run through a fine mesh strainer into a bowl. Add mayo, mustard, and butter. Mix until smooth. Stir in lemon juice. Add cayenne, salt, and pepper to taste. Put in a Ziploc® bag with a cut-off corner.

Fill egg white halves by pressing the bag.

DAVID'S YUMMY DEVILED EGGS

2 peeled hardboiled eggs, halved lengthwise
1 Tbsp. celery
1 Tbsp. Texas sweet onion
Salt
Pepper (or paprika)
1 Tbsp. mayo
1 Tbsp. Dijonaise®

Break down egg yolks. Chop celery and onion very finely. Add salt and pepper (or paprika). Add mayo and Dijonaise® to taste—add slowly and not too much. Spoon mixture into egg white halves.

SOUTHERN LIVING'S DEVILED EGGS

12 hardboiled eggs, peeled
1 ½ Tbsp. Dijon mustard
1 ½ Tbsp. mayonnaise
15 pimiento-stuffed green olives, halved
1 tsp. Tony Chachere's® Creole Seasoning

Cut eggs in half; carefully remove yolks. Mash yolks and stir in mustard and mayo until well-blended.

Spoon mixture into egg white halves. Place olive half in center; sprinkle with seasoning.

DEVILED EGGS WITH CRAB

6 large hardboiled eggs, peeled
2 Tbsp. EVOO
1 tsp. fresh lemon juice
Cayenne pepper
1 Tbsp. finely chopped flat-leaf parsley
1 Tbsp. minced scallion
1 Tbsp. small capers, rinsed
½ lb. lump crabmeat
Salt
Freshly ground pepper
½ tsp. Dijon mustard

Halve eggs lengthwise. Carefully scoop the egg yolks into a bowl. Using a fork, mash the yolks with olive oil, lemon juice, and a generous pinch of cayenne. Stir in the parsley, scallion, and capers. Gently fold in the crab. Season with salt and pepper. Generously mound the filling into the egg-white halves.

CHIVE-TARRAGON EGGS

12 large hardboiled eggs, peeled and halved
½ cup mayo
1 Tbsp. lemon juice
1/8 tsp. Tabasco®
2 Tbsp. finely chopped fresh chives
2 tsp. finely chopped fresh tarragon
½ tsp. salt
½ tsp. dry mustard

Mash egg yolks with mayo, lemon juice, and hot sauce. Add dry ingredients.

Mound filling into egg white halves. Chill at least 1 hour.

CURRIED DEVILED EGGS

8 peeled hardboiled eggs, halved
¼ cup mayonnaise
1 Tbsp. sweet pickle juice
1 tsp. yellow mustard
1 tsp. curry powder
¼ tsp. salt
Pepper

Mash egg yolks. Stir in mayo, pickle juice, and mustard. Add dry ingredients.

Mound filling into egg white halves. Chill at least 1 hour.

Nota bene: All of the above recipes may be transformed into egg salad sandwich spreads. Enjoy!

EGG SALAD WITH VARIATIONS

BASIC RECIPE

> 6-8 medium hardboiled eggs, peeled
> 3 Tbsp. Lite Mayo + 1 Tbsp. plain yogurt, mixed
> Salt and pepper
> 2 medium stalks celery, strings removed and chopped fine

Cut through the eggs and mayo/yogurt mix with a small paring knife until the mix is the proper texture for you. Some like it chunky, some mushy.

Add a couple of generous pinches of salt & pepper and a couple of pinches of any seasoning from the list below. I like curry.

Add celery. Stir with a large spoon until combined. Adjust seasonings to taste.

Sweeter & Fruitier version: Plain yogurt, curry powder, chopped apples, toasted pecans and minced chives.

OR ADD TO ABOVE BASIC RECIPE YOUR CHOICE OR COMBO:

Curry powder	Chopped chives
Chopped green or black olives	Pinch of Wasabi powder
Finely chopped cucumbers or water chestnuts (instead of celery)	
Capers	Salted sunflower seeds
3-4 slices crisp bacon crumbled	Shredded carrots
Dill or sweet pickle chopped fine	Tabasco®
Any kind of mustard	Cream cheese
Dill weed	Finely chopped bell pepper
Paprika	Yogurt (instead of mayo)
Finely chopped spring onions	Cumin
Tony Chachere's ® Creole Seasoning	
Celery seed	

NOTES AND VARIATIONS

HORS D'OEUVRES & NUTS

JACKIE'S BRIE APPETIZER

1 wheel of brie
1 pkg. Pepperidge Farm® frozen puff pastry dough
Major Grey's® mango chutney or apricot preserves
Fresh basil
Fresh rosemary
Egg whites

Preheat oven to 350 degrees.

Place brie of top of one piece of puff pastry. Generously spread apricot preserves across top. Chop equal amounts of basil and rosemary and sprinkle over. Place second piece of puff pastry on top. Trim edges of pastry to fit. Pinch edges, brush with egg whites.

Bake 30 minutes.

JAN'S CHEESE & CHUTNEY YUMYUM

1 8-oz. pkg. lite cream cheese
¼ cup grated cheddar cheese
Salt
Pepper
Chutney
Green onion, chopped
5 pieces bacon, cooked
Parsley, chopped

Combine cream cheese, cheddar cheese, salt, and pepper. Mold, then let set a few hours.

"Frost" cheese mixture with chutney; top with chopped green onions—both bulb and green portions. Add variation of grated cheese. Sprinkle with crumbled bacon. Garnish with parsley.

JAN'S PARMESAN CHEESE BITES

1 cup all-purpose flour
2/3 cup grated Parmesan
¼ tsp. ground red pepper
½ cup butter, cut up
2 Tbsp. milk

In food processor, pulse flour, cheese, pepper, and butter until blended. Shape into two 4-inch logs. Wrap in saran. Put in air-tight container. Chill 8 hours.

Cut log into slices. Place on lightly greased baking sheet. Coat with milk.

Bake 12–15 minutes at 350 degrees.

PARMESAN CRACKERS

1 cup all-purpose flour
1 cup grated Parmigiano-Reggiano cheese
½ cup unsalted butter

Pulse all ingredients until dough comes together. Place mixture onto a piece of saran and form into a log, 1 ½ inches in diameter. Chill at least 2 hours.

Preheat oven to 325 degrees.

Grease two baking sheets. Cut log into ¼-inch slices and place an inch apart. Bake 12–13 minutes.

Remove crackers and raise oven heat to 500 degrees. After it reaches 500, bake 3 additional minutes or until golden brown. Cool on a wire rack.

CHILI CHEESE ROUNDS

    2 lbs. grated sharp cheese
    2 cups pecans
    1 tsp. oregano
    1 large clove of garlic
    5 tsp. mayo
    1 Tbsp. chili powder

Chop ingredients in a food chopper; mix together well.

Separate mixture into 4–5 round balls. Roll balls in chili powder sprinkled on wax paper until well-coated. Cover and store in freezer.

RUMAKI

Ingredients vary.

    Water chestnuts
    Soy sauce
    Bacon

Brush canned water chestnuts, or chicken liver halves, or cut-up Portobello mushrooms, with soy sauce. Wrap in pieces of uncooked bacon. Skewer closed with a toothpick and broil, turning once, until bacon is fully cooked.

TEXAS CAVIAR (PICKLED BLACK-EYED PEAS)

2 pkgs. fresh black-eyed peas
½ thin-sliced onion
3 cloves garlic
1 cup EVOO
Red wine vinegar
Salt
Pepper

Rinse peas and place in saucepan. Cover with water. Bring to a boil and simmer for 15–18 minutes or until done.

Drain and pour into large glass bowl.

While peas are still hot, add sliced onion and whole peeled garlic cloves. May remove garlic after 24 hours.

Add EVOO and several generous sprinkles of red wine vinegar. Add salt and pepper to taste. May be kept as long as 2 weeks in the refrigerator.

SALMON TARTARE

¼ cup capers, drained
8 oz. smoked salmon
2 tsp. chopped fresh dill
2 Tbsp. EVOO
½ tsp. finely grated lemon zest
¼ cup finely diced red onion

Pulse capers until coarsely chopped. Add salmon, dill, EVOO, and zest until the salmon is finely chopped. Stir in red onion.

Makes 1½ cups.

SHRIMP APPETIZER FOR 8

2 lbs. shrimp—cooked, peeled, and deveined
½ cup fresh lemon juice
¼ cup vegetable oil
1 tsp. red wine vinegar
2 garlic cloves, peeled and crushed
1 tsp. dry mustard
2 tsp. salt
½ tsp. paprika
Red pepper flakes
1 bay leaf
1 lemon, thinly sliced
2 small red onions, thinly sliced
2 tsp. chopped fresh parsley

Mix all ingredients together. Marinate shrimp in the refrigerator for 2–4 hours.

Remove bay leaf before serving.

HOMESTYLE PICKLED SHRIMP

3 lbs. shrimp, steamed until pink
2 medium onions, quartered and thinly sliced
6 garlic cloves, thinly sliced
1 tsp. each celery, fennel, mustard, coriander
4 lemons, thinly sliced
1 tsp. freshly ground white pepper
¼ cup white wine vinegar
½ cup freshly squeezed lemon juice
14 whole bay leaves
1 cup EVOO
¼ tsp. pepper flakes
1 cup parsley sprigs

Cook shrimp until pink. Drain. Combine all ingredients in a glass bowl. Refrigerate at least 6 hours or overnight. Remove from the fridge 1 hour before serving.

Remove the bay leaves.

Makes 15–20 servings.

CAROL'S CEVICHE

1 ½ lbs. filleted raw fish
10–12 fresh limes, juiced

Cut fish into quarter-inch cubes. Place into a glass dish and cover with lime juice. The juice must cover the fish; add until fully covered. Let stand overnight in the refrigerator.

SAUCE
Combine:
3 large tomatoes, chopped
4 cups chopped parsley
1 small onion, finely chopped
2 Tbsp. EVOO
Tabasco®
¼ tsp. ground cloves
1 tsp. oregano
1 tsp. salt

Drain fish and rinse in cold water. Add sauce and chill for a least 1 hour. Serve on saltine crackers.

SCALLOPS
Serves 4.

32 medium scallops
1 cup lime juice
1 cup lemon juice
½ tsp. salt
1 tsp. fresh ground pepper
1 clove garlic, minced
1 small red onion, minced
1 small jalapeño—seeded, rinsed,
   and minced
1 cup parsley, minced

MARINATED OLIVES

2 cups assorted olives
2 cloves garlic, peeled and crushed
2 Tbsp. EVOO
1 Tbsp. fresh rosemary
½ lemon, cut in half and segmented like a grapefruit

Toss all ingredients in a bowl. Marinate for at least 1 hour at room temperature. Refrigerate if not using immediately. Remove an hour or two before serving.

MARINATED MUSHROOMS

1 ¼ pounds white mushrooms, stems trimmed
   (Large mushrooms quartered, smaller halved)
3 Tbsp. EVOO
2 Tbsp. fresh squeezed lemon juice
1 bay leaf
1 tsp. black peppercorns
1 tsp. salt
1 medium onion, quartered (layers separated)
½ cup dry white wine
½ Tbsp. thyme leaves
½ Tbsp. coriander

Combine all ingredients and bring to a boil over high heat. Cover and boil for 6 minutes, stirring once or twice. Transfer to a glass bowl and let cool.

Can be made 4 days ahead and refrigerated. Bring to room temperature and remove bay leaf before serving.

MORE MARINATED MUSHROOMS

2 pounds small fresh mushrooms
2/3 cup wine vinegar
½ cup salad oil
2 large cloves garlic, sliced
2 tsp. salt
¼ cup chopped parsley
1 Tbsp. Dijon mustard
2 Tbsp. brown sugar

Wipe mushrooms. Mix all other ingredients and bring to a boil. Add mushrooms. Simmer 15 minutes and allow to cool in liquid. Refrigerate several hours, stirring occasionally. Drain and serve with cocktail picks.

ROASTED LEMON SHELLS

4 lemons, rinsed
2 tsp. sugar
Sea salt
Ground pepper

Preheat oven to 400 degrees.

Wrap lemons in two layers of foil. Place on a sheet or pan. Bake for 1 ½ hours. Let cool, then unwrap.

Cut shells in half and carefully scoop out the flesh. Reserve the lemon halves. Remove seeds by pressing through a strainer. Stir in sugar and season with salt and pepper.

Serve shells filled with pureed lemon flesh and a few tablespoons of tapenade. See recipe below. Eat shells and all.

TAPENADE

2 cups pitted Greek or Moroccan dry-cured olives
3 cloves garlic, peeled and chopped
6 oz. anchovy filets, drained and patted dry
1 6-oz. can good quality tuna in oil, drained
½ cup capers, drained
1 tsp. green peppercorns in brine, drained and chopped
½ tsp. chopped fresh thyme
2 tsp. grated lemon zest
½ cup fresh lemon juice
2/3 cup EVOO

In food processor, pulse all ingredients except oil until just combined. With motor running, add oil slowly. Don't over-process. The tapenade should have some chunkiness.

Refrigerate for later use, or spoon into the lemon shells. Yields 3 cups.

ROASTED PECANS FLORENCE

1 stick butter, melted
Tabasco®
Cayenne
4–5 cups pecan halves
Worcestershire sauce
Salt

Preheat oven to 325 degrees.

Stir butter, Tabasco®, and cayenne to taste, then mix in pecan halves. Put mixture on a flat baking sheet.

Cook for 30–40 minutes, stirring every 10 minutes. Add salt.

ARKANSAS HOT PECANS

1 cup pecans
2 Tbsp. melted butter
2 tsp. soy
6 dashes red pepper sauce
1 tsp. beau monde

Bake pecans at 300 degrees for 25–30 min. Add to seasonings. After 30 minutes, remove pecans and drain on paper towel. Can store in freezer.

MORE PECANS

4–5 cups pecans
½ stick butter, melted
½ tsp. salt
Ground cinnamon
Garlic powder
6 tsp. Worcestershire sauce
3–6 dashes Tabasco® and cayenne pepper

Spread pecans on baking sheet and bake at 350 degrees for 25–30 minutes. Mix other ingredients and stir in pecans. Let stand 30 minutes. Remove pecans and drain on a paper towel. Stores well in freezer.

SPICY PECANS

2 large egg whites

1 ½ tsp. salt

3/4 cup sugar

2 tsp. Worcestershire sauce

2 tsp. paprika

1 ½ tsp. cayenne pepper

4 ½ cups pecan halves
6 Tbsp. unsalted butter, melted

Preheat oven to 325 degrees.

Beat egg whites with salt until foamy. Add sugar, Worcestershire sauce, paprika, and cayenne. Fold in pecans and melted butter. Place in glass baking dish.

Bake 30–40 minutes, stirring every 10 minutes.

NOTES AND VARIATIONS

DIPS,
MARINADES,
DRESSINGS &
SAUCES

JULIE'S HOT ARTICHOKE DIP

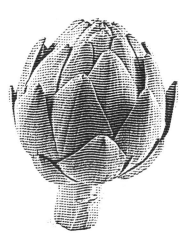

2 jars marinated artichokes
1 small chopped onion
½ lb. cheddar cheese
¼ cup bread crumbs
4 eggs, beaten
Salt
Oregano
Cayenne

Preheat oven to 325 degrees.

Drain oil from one of the artichoke jars. Sauté chopped onion in the oil. Grate ½ pound cheddar. Chop artichokes. Add cheese, bread crumbs, and beaten eggs. Flavor with salt, oregano, and cayenne.

Bake for 30 minutes.

MM'S SPINACH DIP

2 pkg. frozen chopped spinach, thawed and dried
1 pkg. Knorr's® dry vegetable soup mix
½ cup sour cream
½ cup mayonnaise
1 Tbsp. finely chopped onion
Fresh ground pepper
Horseradish
1 unsliced loaf bread

Combine all ingredients except for bread ahead of time, to give mixture a chance to blend. Cut round hole in loaf of bread, fill with mixture, and serve with additional torn bread pieces.

PAUL GILETTE'S SMOKED SALMON DIP

1 brick cream cheese, softened
2 Tbsp. sour cream or plain non-fat yogurt
1 Tbsp. mayonnaise
6 tsp. chopped Vidalia onions
3 green onions, chopped (tops too)
Cracked pepper
1/3 cup chopped smoked salmon

Mix ingredients. Let sit a day for flavors to "marry."

HOT CRAB DIP

½ lb (8 oz) lump crabmeat
½ cup grated Monterey Jack cheese
¼ cup light mayo
2 Tbsp. fat free sour cream
2 Tbsp. grated Parmesan cheese
3 Tbsp. minced green onions
2 Tbsp. minced garlic
1 tsp. Worcestershire sauce
1 tsp. lemon or lime juice
½ tsp. Tabasco®
¼ tsp. dry mustard
Ground black pepper
Salt

Preheat oven to 325 degrees.

Combine all of the ingredients, stirring until well-mixed. Spoon into a large ramekin or small baking dish.

Bake 30 minutes or until bubbly. Makes 2 cups.

CLAM DIP

1 clove garlic, pressed
1 ½ lb. soft cream cheese
1 ½ tsp. Worcestershire sauce
½ tsp. salt
Ground pepper
1 7-oz. tin of minced clams
¼ cup clam broth

Mix all ingredients. Cover. Refrigerate for 3 hours.

BEAN DIP

1 large can refried beans
1 8-oz. pkg. cream cheese
1 large carton sour cream
1 bunch of green onions, chopped
1 pkg. taco seasoning
1 clove garlic, pressed
1 small can green chili peppers
½ cup Pace Picante® sauce
Cayenne
Salt
15 oz. Monterrey Jack, shredded
10 oz. cheddar cheese, shredded

Preheat oven to 300 degrees.

Mix ingredients. Bake for 1 hour.

KISS (KEEP IT SIMPLE, STUPID) DIP

Mix equal parts cream cheese and sour cream. Blend equal parts Hormel® chili and Ortega® salsa. Mix equal parts shredded cheddar and Monterrey Jack cheese. Layer once or twice.

Microwave five minutes.

ERIC FAIRCHILD'S TUNA DIP

    2 cans albacore tuna in water, drained
    1 large pkg. softened cream cheese
    1 onion, grated
    Worcestershire sauce
    1 Tbsp. catsup
    Salt
    Pepper

Mix ingredients. Serve with crackers or bread.

CORN DIP

    2 regular cans of Mexican or plain corn, drained
    1 cup lite mayo
    8 oz. lite or fat-free sour cream
    1 cup finely chopped onion
    1 small can chopped green chilies
    4–6 shakes spicy seasoning salt

Mix ingredients. Refrigerate overnight.

ROASTED EGGPLANT DIP

1 medium eggplant
2 red bell peppers
1 red onion
2 cloves garlic, minced
3 Tbsp. EVOO
1 ½ tsp. kosher salt
½ tsp. ground pepper
1 Tbsp. tomato paste

Preheat oven to 400 degrees.

Cube eggplant, pepper, and onion into 1-inch pieces. Toss in large bowl with rest of the ingredients. Spread on baking sheet.

Roast for 45 minutes. Toss once.

Put in food processor add tomato paste. Pulse to blend. Add additional salt and pepper for taste. Serves 6–8.

HUMMUS

Chickpeas
Tahini
Garlic
Cumin
Pimento
EVOO
Lemon juice
Salt
Pepper

Mix 4 parts well-cooked or canned chickpeas with 1 part tahini, using some of its oil, in a food processor. Add garlic, cumin, and pimento. Purée, adding EVOO as needed. Stir in lemon juice, salt, and pepper to taste. Garnish with additional pimento and EVOO.

MEXICAN DIP

2 cans bean dip or one 16-oz. can refried beans
1 cup sour cream
¼ cup mayo
1 pkg. taco seasoning
3 avocados, peeled and seeded
2 tsp. lime juice
Salt
Pepper
2 tomatoes, chopped
2 bunches green onions, chopped or 1 small onion, chopped
1 4-oz. can chopped green chilies
1 ½ cup Longhorn or Monterey Jack cheese, grated

Use 12" round or square glass dish, 2" deep.

Layer 1:   Spread bean dip or refried beans in the bottom of dish

Mix sour cream, mayo, taco seasonings. Mash avocados and spoon sour cream mixture over the avocados.

Layer 2:   Add lime juice, salt, and pepper to mashed avocado mixture.

Layer 3:   See above (these three steps can be done several days beforehand). Take out of refrigerator 30 minutes before sprinkling the fourth layer.

Layer 4:   Combine tomatoes, onions, and chopped green chilies.

Layer 5:   Add grated cheese.

Let sit overnight. Serve with Fritos©.

GERI'S PORK TENDER MARINADE

1 Tbsp. sherry
2 Tbsp. brown sugar
2 Tbsp. soy sauce (lite)
½ tsp. cinnamon
½ tsp. salt

Combine liquid ingredients. Rub cinnamon and salt into tender. Marinate in refrigerator overnight.

TED A'S STEAK AND LAMB MARINADE

French's® Yellow mustard
Garlic pepper or pepper
Salt-less garlic salt

Mix ingredients and marinate lamb overnight.

LAMB MARINADE

3 large cloves garlic
1 onion, quartered
½ jalapeño pepper, seeded
1- square inch piece fresh ginger root, peeled
¼ cup soy sauce
¼ cup honey
2 Tbsp. vegetable oil

Puree garlic, onion, jalapeño pepper, and ginger root in mixer. Add soy sauce, honey, and vegetable oil.

PETE'S PORK LOIN MARINADE

Balsamic vinegar
Worcestershire sauce
Crushed garlic cloves

Mix ingredients and marinate meat overnight.

MASEY'S FLANK STEAK MARINADE

5 Tbsp. Dijon mustard
1 tsp. Worcestershire sauce
3–4 Tbsp. low-sodium soy
1 garlic clove, crushed
1 tsp. tarragon
Vermouth

Mix first five ingredients in a bowl. Add vermouth to thicken consistency to that of a chowder. Put meat and marinade in large plastic bag and marinate in refrigerator overnight.

MARK WEBSTER'S MARINADE SAUCE FOR VENISON

3/4 cup vegetable oil
4 Tbsp. cider vinegar
3 Tbsp. brown sugar
3 Tbsp. Worcestershire sauce
2 Tbsp. soy sauce
1 bottle Heinz® chili sauce

Mix all ingredients. Marinate overnight.

QUICK BRINE FOR PORK CHOPS

Rub chops with salt and herbs. Let sit at room temperature for a couple of hours. Rub with a bit of EVOO and pepper.

TANDOORI MARINADE FOR CHICKEN OR MEAT

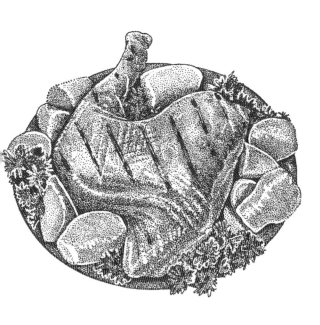

2-inch cube fresh ginger, chopped
3 garlic cloves, chopped
½ medium onion, chopped
3 tsp. lemon juice with pulp

Mix ingredients in blender to make a paste,
then add:
1 cup low-fat yogurt
1 tsp. cumin
1 tsp. coriander
½ tsp. cinnamon
½ tsp. turmeric
½ tsp. cayenne pepper
2 tsp. salt
4 Tbsp. EVOO

Skin chicken. For both chicken and meat, perforate the pieces and cut into them slightly. Massage the marinade into the meat.

Marinate in the fridge for 24 hours.

Cook over a hot, covered fire.

DUCK BREAST MARINADE

Dried thyme
1 tsp. soy
1 Tbsp. grain mustard

Mix ingredients. Marinate 30 minutes. Cut into skin. Sauté.

RUB FOR FRIED CHICKEN

Buttermilk
Chicken
Salt
Pepper
Paprika
Flour

After soaking chicken in buttermilk for at least 2 hours, roll chicken in mixture of salt, pepper, paprika, and flour before frying.

OLIVE OIL AND BASALMIC VINEGAR DRESSING

Follow directions for making 1 package of Good Seasons® Italian dressing with EVOO and balsamic vinegar.

Great combo: crisp romaine, crumbled blue cheese, salt, and pepper to taste.

RITTER'S VINAIGRETTE DRESSING

¼ cup vinegar
½ cup EVOO
2 cloves garlic
2 Tbsp. Dijon mustard
¼ tsp. salt

Whip ingredients together. Serve as dressing.

DICK DELMARLE'S VINAIGRETTE DRESSING

2 cups vegetable oil
1 cup cider vinegar
1 ½ tsp. salt
½ tsp. pepper
1 tsp. Colman's® dry mustard
Grated onion

Mix ingredients. Toss into salad until it spreads throughout.

CLASSIC VINAIGRETTE DRESSING

1 rounded tsp. Dijon mustard
2 Tbsp. red wine vinegar
1 scant tsp. fresh lemon juice
¼ tsp. salt
5 twists of a peppermill
¼ cup EVOO
2 Tbsp. vegetable oil

Combine all ingredients except oils, then whisk to dissolve the salt. Gradually whisk in the olive oil, then the vegetable oil, in a very thin stream.

Makes enough for 10–12 cups of salad greens.

SHELLFISH MAYONNAISE

1 cup mayo
1 Tbsp. Dijon mustard
1 tsp. tarragon vinegar
1 tsp. chopped cilantro
2 tsp. drained tiny capers
1 scallion with 3" green left on, thinly sliced
¼ tsp. Tabasco®
Salt
Pepper

Mix ingredients and serve.

OTHER MAYONNAISE THOUGHTS

You may add lemon, lime, vinegar, sour cream, or yogurt to thin your mayo if need be.

Start with 1cup mayo and add one or more of the following:

1 tsp. finely minced garlic
Mild chili powder
Dijon or whole grain mustard
Curry
Chopped pickles
Tabasco®
Capers
Anchovies
Soy

Adjust to taste and enjoy.

NO-BRAIN HOLLANDAISE

6 egg yolks
3 tsp. lemon juice
3 sticks melted butter
Salt
Pepper

Blend eggs and lemon juice in food processor. Add butter s l o w l y. Season with salt and pepper to taste.

RÉMOULADE SAUCE

2 Tbsp. Zatarain's® mustard
1 tsp. paprika
½ tsp. cayenne
1 ½ tsp. salt
¼ cup tarragon vinegar
½ cup plus 3 Tbsp. EVOO
3/4 chopped scallions
¼ cup minced parsley
¼ cup chopped cilantro

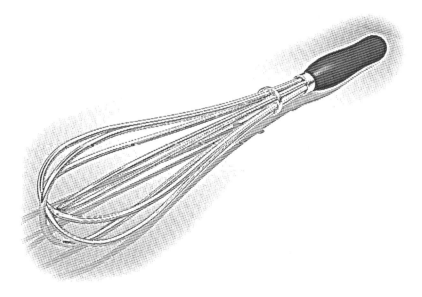

Whisk together mustard, paprika, cayenne, and salt. Beat in vinegar. Add oil in slow stream, whisking constantly. Add scallions, parsley, and cilantro; mix well. Cover tightly with plastic wrap and let rest at room temperature for 4 hours.

BASIC BARBEQUE SAUCE

1 cup melted butter
½ cup granulated sugar
½ tsp. cayenne pepper
1 Tbsp. prepared mustard
2 cups salad oil
2 bottles catsup
2/3 cup Worcestershire sauce
4 cloves garlic, minced
½ cup onion, minced
½ cup lemon juice
½ Tbsp. Tabasco®

Stir sugar into melted butter. Add remaining ing
ered, stirring occasionally. Refrigerate.

CURRY SAUCE FOR SHRIMP, CHICKEN, OR LAMB

Recipe serves 16–20.

1 cup minced onion
   1 cup butter
   1 tsp. salt
   5 tsp. curry to taste
   ½ tsp. ground ginger
   3/4 cup flour
   5 cups milk
   2 cups cream
   ½ cup sherry
   Meat of choice

Sauté onions in butter until onions are yellow. Add salt, curry powder, and ginger. Mix thoroughly. Add flour slowly and cook until bubbly. Add milk and cream, stirring briskly until smooth and thick and all starchy flavor has disappeared. Add sherry and the cooked meat.

CONDIMENTS:
    Chutney
    Bacon bits
    Browned coconut
    Finely chopped browned almonds
    Chopped tomatoes
    Slivered ripe olives
    Pineapple chunks
    Chopped sweet pickle
    Chopped avocado
    Finely chopped egg yolks and egg whites (separate)

SAUCE FOR COLD MEATS

    ½ tsp. salt
    1 Tbsp. Dijon mustard
    1 Tbsp. wine vinegar
    3 Tbsp. EVOO
    1 Tbsp. capers
    2 cornichon pickles, chopped
    1 hardboiled egg, chopped fine
    1 Tbsp. fresh parsley
    Freshly ground pepper

Mix all ingredients. Hold back adding the parsley until right before serving. Taste and adjust seasonings to get the balance right.

Makes 3/4 cup, enough to dress meats for 3–4 servings.

NOTES AND VARIATIONS

SALADS

TO REHYDRATE LETTUCE

Fill a bowl with room temperature water. Soak lettuce. After a few minutes plunge lettuce into iced water. The lettuce will immediately crisp. Pat dry.

MOROCCAN BEET SALAD

6–8 fresh medium beets
Juice of one lemon
2 cloves garlic, minced
1 tsp. cumin
Salt
Black pepper
4 Tbsp. EVOO
½ cup diced parsley

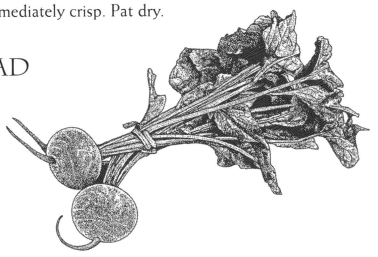

Cook beets about 45 minutes. Cool, peel, and cut into bite-sized pieces. Or buy the canned equivalent, or enough to serve six. Set aside in a serving bowl.

Mix lemon juice, garlic, cumin, salt, and pepper in a small bowl. Whisk in EVOO, then toss with beets. Let sit a few hours. Just before serving, sprinkle with parsley.

ANDREA'S BROCCOLI COLESLAW

1 bag Mann's® broccoli coleslaw
½ cup sliced almonds, toasted
½ cup sunflower seeds
1 pkg. ramen noodle soup, chicken flavor
DRESSING:
½ cup vegetable or canola oil
3 Tbsp. red wine vinegar
2 Tbsp. sugar
1 tsp. salt

Combine and mix all but the dressing. Break up noodles. Add seasoning packet from ramen noodles. Toss.

NANCY POWER'S BROCCOLI SALAD

4 cups broccoli florets "al dente"
1 cup chopped green onions
1 cup green seedless grapes
1 cup red seedless grapes
1 cup celery, chopped fine
Medium package slivered toasted almonds

Dress with:
1 cup mayo
2 tsp. rice vinegar
Sugar

Toss vegetables. Mix dressing ingredients.

Add sugar (or sugar substitute) to taste.

Combine and serve.

CUCUMBER SALAD

Cucumbers
Salt
White pepper
Mint
Vinegar
EVOO

Slit and seed cucumbers. Slice thinly. Add salt and white pepper, then add chopped mint. Slowly add white vinegar and EVOO until cucumbers are lightly covered.

PETE & ANDREA'S CORN SALAD FOR 12

8 cups canned corn, drained and rinsed
1 large seeded red pepper, cut into ½" dices
1 large seeded green pepper, cut into ½" dices
½ pint cherry tomatoes, halved
1 cucumber—peeled, seeded, and chopped
Dill
1 cup finely chopped red onion
3/4 cup EVOO
¼ cup balsamic vinegar
Salt
Fresh ground pepper

Combine corn, red and green bell peppers, tomatoes, cucumber, dill, and onion. Add olive oil. Toss together. Add vinegar. Continue tossing well to combine. Season to taste with salt and pepper. Marinate one to two hours.

SUCCOTASH SALAD FOR 10

2 pkg. frozen corn
2 pkg. frozen lima beans
3 medium tomatoes—peeled, seeded, and chopped
½ cup basil, coarsely chopped
3 Tbsp. lime juice
4 Tbsp. EVOO
1 Tbsp. Dijon mustard
Salt
Pepper

Let frozen vegetables thaw. Combine vegetables and basil in a large bowl.

Whisk together lime juice, olive oil, mustard, salt, and pepper until emulsified. Pour over vegetables and toss.

Toss again before serving.

FANTASTIC LAYERED SALAD FOR 10–12

Note: Keep greens dry. It is best made the day before.
    Layer One:
    1 bag of spinach, torn
    Salt
    Pepper
    ½ tsp. sugar
    ½ lb. cooked, crumbled bacon
    Cover with avocado slices or 6 hardboiled eggs, sliced.

    Layer Two:
    1 head iceberg, torn
    Salt
    Pepper
    ½ tsp. sugar
    1 box frozen peas, thawed and drained
    1 red onion, sliced and sprinkled with sugar

Cover with sliced raw mushrooms.

Sprinkle with ground black pepper.

Topping: Combine 1 cup sour cream and 2 cups mayo.

Spread over salad until sealed .

Sprinkle grated Jarlsberg or Swiss on top.

Sprinkle with paprika for color.

LAYERED SOUTHWEST SALAD FOR 6–8

2 cup shredded lettuce
1 large avocado
1 16-oz. can black beans, drained
1 10-oz. pkg. frozen corn, thawed (or equivalent can of corn, drained)
10 cherry tomatoes, halved

Layer vegetables.

Combine and spread to seal bowl:
½ cup sour cream
½ cup finely chopped seeded red pepper
½ cup finely chopped seeded green pepper
1 tsp. dried oregano
½ tsp. garlic powder
Salt
Pepper

ISABEL'S CHICKEN SALAD

2 cups diced chicken
2 cups fresh fruit
2 cups chilled, cooked rice
3/4 cups mayo
Juice of 4 limes
Curry powder
Salt
Pepper
2 green onions, chopped
2 Tbsp. slivered almonds

Mix all ingredients except for almonds. Top with almonds.

JAYNE'S SPINACH & STRAWBERRY SALAD

1 package baby spinach, sorted through
1 box small strawberries, "topped"
1 small red onion, sliced thin

Marinate berries and onion in Good Seasons® salad dressing and balsamic vinegar for a few minutes, then toss with spinach.

Note: You can also use a sweeter dressing.

SOUTHERN LIVING'S POTATO SALAD

3 pounds red potatoes
1/3 cup EVOO
2 Tbsp. fresh lemon juice
2 Tbsp. mayonnaise
1 tsp. dried oregano
1 tsp. dry mustard
1 tsp. salt
3 green onions, chopped
½ seeded red bell pepper, finely chopped
2 Tbsp. chopped parsley
½ tsp. black pepper
Salt

Cover potatoes with water. Bring to a boil and cook 20 minutes or until tender. Drain and cool. Cut potatoes into 1-inch pieces.

Stir together olive oil, lemon juice, mayo, oregano, mustard, and salt in a large bowl, blending well. Add potatoes, onions, and remaining ingredients, gently tossing to coat.

Serve at room temperature or chilled.

Serves 8–10.

VIRGINIA'S POTATO SALAD

Recipe serves 8–10.
 1 sack (5 lbs.) small red or salt potatoes
 1 cup Good Seasons® Italian dressing
 1 lb. fresh mushrooms, quartered
 1 pkg. defrosted green peas
 1 medium seeded green pepper, chopped
 1 stalk celery, diced
 1 yellow onion, chopped
 3 tsp. chopped parsley

Boil potatoes. Marinate in Italian dressing. Combine remaining ingredients and mix well.

POTATO SALAD WITH GHERKINS

 1 ½ lbs. red, gold, or white potatoes—scrubbed and diced large
 ½ cup halved and thinly sliced small gherkins
 1 ½ Tbsp. white wine vinegar
 1 ½ Tbsp. vermouth
 2 stalks celery, thinly sliced
 4 green onions, thinly sliced
 ¾ cup low-fat mayo
 Salt
 Pepper

Put potatoes in steamer over salted cold water. Bring to a boil and cook 25–30 minutes.

Drain potatoes. Cool. Add pickles, vinegar, vermouth, celery, onions, and low-fat mayo. Season with salt and pepper. Fold the salad together until well-blended.

ANDREA'S MIXED TOMATO SALAD

Recipe serves 4. Triple to serve 12.

    1 pint cherry tomatoes
    1 pint yellow tomatoes
    1 small red onion, finely diced
    1 clove garlic, minced
    ¼ cup fresh basil, chopped
    ¼ cup fresh cilantro, chopped

Halve the tomatoes. Mix with onion and garlic. Stir in basil and cilantro. Season with salt and pepper. Serve.

BARBARA'S LAYERED TOMATO SALAD

Recipe serves 6.

Combine in a bowl:
    1 tsp. salt
    ½ tsp. dried basil
    ¼ tsp. pepper
    1 clove garlic, minced
    3 Tbsp. cider vinegar
    6 Tbsp. EVOO
    ½ cup chopped parsley
Pour mixture over:
    4 tomatoes, peeled and sliced
    2 cucumbers—peeled, seeded, and sliced
    1 red onion, sliced

Layer tomatoes, red onion, and cucumbers. Cover and refrigerate several hours.

GERI'S BLUE CHEESE COLESLAW

Recipe serves 8.

  2 lbs. cabbage, sliced
  8 oz. blue cheese, crumbled
  1/3 cup cider vinegar
  ¼ tsp. dry mustard
  1 ½ tsp. celery seed
  2 cloves garlic, minced
  ½ tsp. salt
  Pepper
  2 tsp. sugar
  ¼ cup minced onion
  3/4 cup vegetable oil

In large bowl toss cabbage and blue cheese together. Chill for one hour.

Whisk together: vinegar, mustard, celery seed, garlic, salt, pepper, sugar, and onion. Add vegetable oil in a slow, steady stream. Whisk until emulsified. Chill for one hour.

Just before serving, toss cabbage and dressing together.

JACK'S SOUR SLAW

Recipe serves 2.

  Half a head of cabbage
  Celery seed or celery salt
  Salt
  Pepper
  2 Tbsp. cider vinegar
  2 Tbsp. EVOO

Slice cabbage. Mix remaining ingredients. Coat cabbage with mixture, then serve.

CLAIRE'S RICE, PINTO BEAN, AND CORN SALAD

Recipe serves 8–10.

    1 cup rice
    1 ½ cups fresh corn kernels (2 ears)
    2 Tbsp. red wine vinegar
    1 peeled garlic clove, pressed
    2/3 cup EVOO
    Salt and pepper
    1 15 ½ -oz. can pinto beans, rinsed and drained
    2 cups halved cherry tomatoes
    4 green onions, chopped
    1 red bell pepper, chopped
    2 tsp. chopped fresh oregano

Bring 2 cups salted water to a boil in a medium saucepan. Add rice. Reduce to low and cook until rice is tender and water is absorbed, about 20 minutes. Stir in corn. Remove from heat and let stand covered for 5 minutes. Transfer rice with corn to strainer. Rinse to cool.

Whisk vinegar and garlic in a large bowl. Gradually add oil. Season to taste with salt and pepper.

Add remaining ingredients and toss to combine. Let stand at room temperature for at least 30 minutes. Can be made a day ahead and refrigerated. Bring to room temperature before serving.

PATSY'S COLD PASTA SALAD

12 oz. spaghetti
2 Tbsp. Lawry's® Seasoned Salt
4 Tbsp. canola oil
3 Tbsp. fresh lemon juice
1 cup mayo

Cook spaghetti, broken into fourths. Use no salt or any oil. Drain and rinse well.

Add season salt, canola oil, and fresh lemon juice. Mix. Cover and refrigerate overnight.

Add mayo and any or all of the following ingredients:

1 small jar green olives, chopped
1 small can black olives, chopped
1 jar pimientos, chopped
1 cup celery, chopped
1 cup seeded red pepper, chopped
1 small finely diced onion

Serve cold.

PINTO BEAN SALAD

Recipe serves 6.

> 3 cups beans
> 3 Tbsp. finely minced onions
> 1 large garlic clove, pureed and mashed with ¼ tsp. salt
> 3 Tbsp. EVOO or vegetable oil
> Mix of thyme, oregano, and sage
> Pepper
> Red onion rings

Home-cooked beans are preferable, but if you use canned, turn the cans into a sieve and run cold water over them. Whichever beans you use, first toss them gently in a warm chicken stock liquid.

Combine remaining ingredients. Toss beans in mixture and let stand at least 30 minutes, folding gently several more times. Season to taste. Serve topped with red onion rings.

JACKIE'S FIELD GREENS SALAD WITH SPICY PECANS

Mix a proportionate amount of:
> Field greens
> Crumbled blue cheese
> Chopped green onions
> Sliced granny smith apples, bite sized
> Spicy pecans (See recipe on page 37)

Dressing:
> 2/3 cup sugar
> 1 tsp. dry mustard
> 2/3 cup distilled white vinegar
> 3 Tbsp. apple cider vinegar 4 ½ Tbsp. onion juice
> 2 Tbsp. Worcestershire sauce
> 1 cup vegetable oil

Combine sugar, mustard, and vinegars. Stir until sugar dissolves. Whisk in onion juice and Worcestershire sauce. Add oil s l o w l y, whisking continuously until blended.

NEW YORK TIMES TUNA SALAD

1 12-oz. can solid albacore tuna in water
½ cup Hellman's® mayo
4 large ribs celery, peeled and finely chopped
3 hardboiled eggs, chopped
3 tsp. chopped sweet pickles with their juice
1 tsp. minced onion
1 tsp. celery salt
1 tsp. McCormick® season-salt
6 dashes Tabasco®
Cracked pepper

Mix ingredients. Let sit at least one hour. Yields about 3 cups.

ANNE R'S FRENCH BREAD

Preheat oven to 325 degrees.
1 loaf French bread, cut in half lengthwise
Mix:
1/3 cup Parmesan cheese
½ cup minced onion
¾ cup mayonnaise
¼ tsp. fresh ground pepper
1 Tbsp. Worcestershire sauce

Spread mixture on bread.
Bake at 325 degrees until lightly browned.

ELVIS' FAVORITE CORN BREAD

Recipe serves 8.

1 tsp. oil
2 cups cornmeal
1 cup all-purpose flour
1 Tbsp. baking powder
1 ½ Tbsp. sugar
2 ½ cups buttermilk
3 eggs
¼ cup oil

In a 10-inch nonstick skillet, sprinkle oil and cornmeal. Heat.

In a bowl, mix remaining ingredients together and pour into the skillet. Cook until golden brown.

FLORENCE'S JALAPEÑO CORNBREAD

Recipe serves 6–8.
1 cup yellow corn meal
1 cup buttermilk
½ tsp. baking soda
1 cup cream style corn

2 eggs
1 tsp. salt
3 jalapeños, seeded and chopped fine
1 cup green onions, cut fine
½ cup oil or 4 Tbsp. bacon grease
½ lb. grated cheddar cheese or Monterrey Jack

IN A HEAVY SKILLET—Preheat oven to 350 degrees.

Mix all ingredients together except oil and ½ of the cheese. Put oil or bacon grease in bottom of pan. Be sure it covers the bottom completely. Heat pan over stovetop until oil is hot or bacon grease melts. Pour batter into skillet. Stir fast to melt cheese.

Put skillet in oven and bake for 30–40 minutes.

IN THE OVEN—Preheat oven to 400 degrees.

Follow above instructions but add all the cheese.

Use a 10x15-inch baking pan. Warm pan in oven for about 5 minutes. Remove and pour in batter.

Bake for about 30 minutes.

NOTES AND VARIATIONS

SOUPS

BASIC CREAMY VEGETABLE SOUP

Recipe serves 6–8.
  2 Tbsp. olive oil
  1 ½ lbs. vegetables of your choice, cut into 1-inch chunks
  (or prepared as described in variations below)
  1 large onion, diced large
  1 Tbsp. butter
  1 large pinch of sugar
  3 large garlic cloves, thickly sliced
  Dried herbs and/or spices as needed
  3 cups chicken broth
  1–1½ cups half & half
  Salt
  Freshly ground pepper

Heat oil over medium-high heat in a large, deep saucepan until simmering. Add vegetable of choice, then onion.

Sauté, stirring very little at first, then more frequently until the vegetables start to turn golden brown, approximately 7 to 8 minutes. Reduce heat to low and add butter, sugar, and garlic. Keep cooking the vegetables about 10 minutes longer. Add herbs and spices and cook between 30 seconds and 1 minute. Reduce heat to low and simmer, partially covered, until the vegetables are tender, about ten minutes.

Using an immersion blender, purée until smooth, about 30 seconds or 1 minute. Add enough half & half so the mixture is soupy, yet thick enough to float garnish. Add salt and pepper to taste. Heat, ladle, garnish, and serve.

Potato soup: Add 4 to 5 cups peeled russet potatoes and 1 ½ tsp. minced fresh rosemary. Garnish with crumbled bacon.

Butternut squash soup: Add 5 cups peeled and seeded butternut squash. Add 1 ½ tsp. cinnamon, 1 tsp. ground ginger, ¼ tsp. ground cloves, and 1/8 tsp. cayenne pepper. Garnish with store-bought apple chips.

Carrot with curry soup: Add 4 to 5 cups peeled carrots and 2 Tbsp. curry powder. Garnish with chopped, roasted pistachios.

Beet soup: Add 4 cups raw beets plus a scant tsp. ground toasted caraway seeds. (To toast: Heat ½ tsp. seeds in a small skillet over medium-low heat until they start to gently pop. Cool and crush with a rolling pin.) Add 1/8 tsp. cayenne pepper and 2 Tbsp. fresh dill.

Turnip soup: Add 5 cups peeled turnips, 2 tsp. paprika, 1 tsp. dried thyme leaves, and 1/8 tsp. cayenne pepper.

Cauliflower soup: Use one small head cut into large florets or 6 heaping cups cauliflower. Add 1 tsp. ground ginger, ½ tsp. ground turmeric, 1/8 tsp. saffron threads, and ½ tsp. cayenne pepper.

CHICKEN SOUP FOR 4

    1 box (4 cups) organic chicken broth
    ½ cup rice
    4 to 5 cloves garlic, crushed
    2 to 3 lemons
    1 can corn, no salt or sugar added
    1 can white chicken meat

Pour chicken broth into a soup pot. Add rice and garlic. Boil about 10 minutes or until the rice is almost cooked. Squeeze juice from the lemons into a bowl and remove the seeds. Turn down the heat and add the drained corn, chicken, and lemon juice. Blend, while leaving some texture.

MM'S COLD TOMATO COBB SOUP BISBY

Recipe serves 6.
>   6 large ripe tomatoes
>   1 white onion, chopped
>   ¼ tsp. fresh ground pepper
>   4 tsp. herbs (basil, tarragon, and dill soaked in water)

Peel tomatoes and mix with onion and seasonings. Refrigerate.

May be done 2 days before use.

>   Optional topping:
>   5 Tbsp. non-fat yogurt or mayo
>   4 tsp. minced parsley
>   1 tsp. curry powder

Mix and refrigerate. Then spoon it onto tomato soup.

GERI'S CLAM CHOWDER FOR 12

>   3 slices bacon, cooked crisp and crumbled
>   2 tsp. drippings
>   ½ cup chopped green onions
>   8 oz. low-fat cream cheese
>   4 small cans clams, drain (save broth)
>   1 can creamed corn
>
>   1 can regular corn
>   3 cans cream of potato soup
>   1 can cream of celery soup
>   1 soup can of milk
>   1 flat tsp. cayenne pepper
>   1 cup chopped celery
>   2 cups grated carrots

Use bacon drippings to sauté onions. Place cream cheese in clam broth to soften.

Mix all ingredients together and simmer on low for 20–30 minutes.

Note: Use low-fat soups, cream cheese, and skim milk.

JULIE'S CLAM CHOWDER FOR 8

4 cans Campbell's® Clam Chowder
2 cups half & half
1 cup milk
½ stick butter
2 cans drained minced clams
Freshly ground pepper
Sherry or Worcestershire sauce
Optional: 1 can of corn, drained

Dilute clam chowder with half & half. Mix all ingredients and bring to a boil. Goes great with spinach salad and rolls for a light supper.

LULU'S GAZPACHO

Recipe makes 2 qts.

12 medium chopped tomatoes
4 chopped small cucumbers
3/4 cup chopped onion
1 bell pepper, chopped
¼ tsp. nutmeg
1/8 tsp. ground cloves
1 tsp. mustard seed
1 cup red wine vinegar
Optional: Add V-8® juice to thin

Mix ingredients. Serve with curried non-fat yogurt or light mayo.

LULU'S FAST, FAST, FAST GAZPACHO

1 tomato, chopped
¼ onion, chopped
¼ tsp. mustard seed
Dash nutmeg
½ cucumber, peeled and chopped
Several dashes red wine vinegar
Couple squirts liquid sweetener

Mix ingredients and serve.

TIP: Knorr's® vegetable soup is easy to make and tastes terrific. Add a little less water than the recipe calls for to enhance taste.

BARBARA'S "EASY AS PIE" TOMATO SOUP

Recipe serves 4.
    2 cans Campbell's® tomato bisque soup
    1 pkg. Knorr's® tomato basil soup mix
    1 can milk
    1 can half & half

Mix ingredients, following recipe on Knorr's® soup mix. Use a little less than the amount of water called for in Knorr's® recipe.

Optional: serve with a dollop of sour cream laced with dill.

GARLIC BROTH

Makes 8 cups.

> 3 small heads garlic
> 1 Tbsp. EVOO
> 9 cups water
> Salt and fresh ground pepper

Smash garlic heads, separating into cloves. Smash and peel cloves. Remove green germ from the center. In a medium saucepan, warm oil over low heat. Stir in garlic and cook, stirring often for 20 minutes, or until the outside is translucent and the garlic is soft. Do not let garlic brown.

Add 9 cups of water and bring to a boil. Lower heat and simmer for 40 minutes. Add salt and fresh ground pepper to taste.

GARLIC SOUP

Recipe serves 4.

> 3 Tbsp. EVOO
> 4 whole garlic bulbs, peeled and thinly sliced
> 2 tsp. thyme leaves
> 6 cups chicken stock
> Salt
> Freshly ground pepper
> 2 large eggs
> 1 Tbsp. white wine vinegar

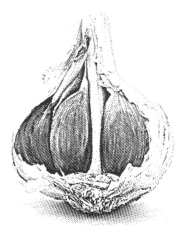

In a large saucepan over medium heat, heat olive oil and add garlic and thyme. Sauté until garlic is soft and translucent, about 6 minutes.

Add stock and bring to a boil over high heat. Simmer until liquid is reduced by half, about 15 minutes. Season to taste with salt and pepper.

In a small bowl combine eggs and vinegar. Beat with a fork until well-blended. Whisk into soup and stir until soup has thickened.

GARLIC SOUP FOR 2

2 cloves garlic
1 bay leaf
1 Tbsp. olive oil
2 cups broth
Salt
Pepper
Dash of Tabasco®
2 egg yolks
4 small pieces toast

Put crushed garlic into a pot with bay leaf and olive oil. Pour boiling broth into pot. Add salt, pepper, and Tabasco®. Boil soup 10 minutes. Take pot off stove.

Place egg yolks in a serving bowl and stir in half a ladle of soup until mixture is smooth. Add to rest of broth. Drop toast into soup and serve.

Can poach an egg in 1 ½ cups of hot mixture until white is set.

CARROT & APPLE SOUP FOR 4

4 Tbsp. chopped onion
2 Tbsp. chopped leeks
2 medium apples—peeled, cored, and sliced
1 ½ cups sliced carrots
2 ½ cups vegetable stock
¼ cup skim milk
2 tsp. minced fresh ginger
Pinch ground cinnamon

In a medium saucepan over low heat, sauté 2 Tbsp. onion, leeks, apple, and carrots for 2 minutes. Add stock and continue to cook for 15–20 minutes or until tender enough to puree.

Add milk, remaining 2 Tbsp. onion, ginger, and cinnamon. Mix well.

Serve warm or chill for one hour.

CHILLED MADRILÈNE WITH SALMON CAVIAR

2 cans madrilène
2 jars red salmon caviar
Mayonnaise
Lemon juice

Chill madrilène until slightly thickened. Gently fold in caviar and chill 4–6 hours. Top with mayo and lemon juice.

CHILLED AVOCADO SOUP

1 can chicken consommé
1 chopped avocado
½ cup light cream
1 finely chopped onion
1 tsp. salt and pepper
3 Tbsp. Worcestershire sauce
2 cups milk

Combine ingredients. Blend, strain, and chill.

AVOCADO SENEGALESE FOR 4

1 can condensed cream of chicken soup
1 soup can of water
½ cup light cream
¼ cup applesauce
2 Tbsp. grated coconut
1 tsp. curry powder
½ tsp. garlic salt
½ tsp. onion powder
1 avocado

In a saucepan, combine all ingredients except the avocado. Heat, stirring occasionally. Halve avocado lengthwise. Discard seed. Slice flesh crosswise. Top each serving with avocado.

CURRY-TOMATO SOUP FOR 4

2 Tbsp. unsalted butter
1 small onion, finely chopped
3 tsp. curry powder
1 tsp. sweet paprika
2 ¼ cup canned Italian plum tomatoes pureed with their juice
2 cups garlic broth
1 tsp. salt
1 Tbsp. fresh lemon juice
Fresh ground pepper
8 Tbsp. plain yogurt

In medium saucepan, melt butter over low heat. Stir in onion and cook until limp, about 10 minutes. Stir in curry powder and paprika, stirring constantly for about 10 minutes. Stir in tomato sauce and broth. Simmer for 5 minutes. Stir in salt. Refrigerate for two hours or overnight if serving cold, or reheat.

Before serving, stir in lemon juice and pepper. Top each serving with 2 Tbsp. yogurt.

NORTH CAROLINA FENNEL AND PEAR SOUP

2 fennel bulbs
2 Tbsp. butter
3 ripe pears
3 3/4 cup chicken stock
2/3 cup sour cream
Salt
Pepper

Trim fennel and chop coarsely. Sauté in butter until soft, about 5 minutes. Peel, core, and chop pears; add to fennel. Add stock. Bring to boil. Simmer for 15 minutes. Puree mix in blender and chill. Garnish with sour cream. Season with salt and pepper to taste.

CORN CHOWDER FOR 2

2 slices bacon
2 Tbsp. onion, chopped
1 can cream of potato soup
1 can creamed corn
1 can milk

Cut up bacon and brown in a saucepan, then remove when cooked. Brown chopped onion; drain off grease. Add cream of potato soup, creamed corn, and milk. Heat and garnish with crumbled bacon.

BLACK BEAN SOUP

Recipe makes 1 gallon.
    1 cup black beans
    2 medium onions, diced
    2 tsp. garlic, chopped
    10 plum tomatoes, roughly chopped
    2 cups bacon, diced
    1 bay leaf
    1 jalapeño, chopped
    1 gallon chicken stock
    Salt
    Pepper
    1 bottle dark beer

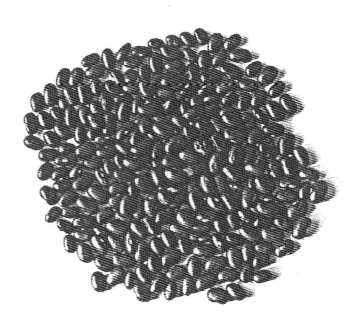

In a soup pot, combine all of the ingredients except the dark beer. Bring the stock to boil. Cover and simmer over low heat until beans are tender, approximately 3 hours.

Just before serving, add beer and bring to near boil for 3 minutes until alcohol evaporates.

Garnish with any of the following:
    1 red onion, diced
    1 tsp. lime juice
    1 tsp. minced jalapeño
    1 large bunch cilantro, chopped

Mix and salt and pepper to taste. Optional: Add a small dollop of non-fat yogurt.

GERI'S TORTILLA SOUP FOR 12

3 onions, chopped
6 jalapeño peppers, seeded and chopped
6 garlic cloves, minced
3 cans (14 ½ oz.) stewed tomatoes
1 chopped avocado
12 cups chicken stock
3 cans tomato soup
3 tsp. cumin
3 tsp. chili powder
1 ½ tsp. lemon pepper
6 tsp. Worcestershire sauce

Sauté onion, jalapeño, garlic, and tomatoes in large kettle for several minutes. Add remaining ingredients and simmer for one hour. Place garnishes in bowls and ladle hot soup on top.

Garnish with:
    Chopped avocado
    Shredded Monterrey Jack
    Chopped cilantro
    Doritos®

MEME'S TACO SOUP FOR 12

1 lb. ground beef
1 onion, chopped
1 32-oz. or 3 12-oz. cans Italian tomatoes
1 green bell pepper, chopped
1 can pinto beans with juice
1 can whole kernel corn with juice
1 can hominy with juice
1 8-oz. can tomato paste
1 pkg. taco seasoning mix
1 pkg. Hidden Valley® ranch dry mix
3 cups water
1 can chicken broth

Brown meat with onions and bell pepper. Drain fat. Chop tomatoes into bite-sized pieces. Add tomatoes and remaining ingredients to the mix. Bring to a boil.

Simmer 1–2 hours. Keeps well in fridge.

GOLDEN DOOR POTASSIUM BROTH

Makes 12 4-oz. servings and can be easily halved.
46 oz. tomato-based vegetable juice, low sodium
2 cups water
1 tsp. chili pepper flakes
1 tsp. dried basil
3 cups vegetable trimmings: celery tops, mushrooms, zucchini, onion, green onion, bell pepper, parsley stems, lettuce, carrots

Combine above ingredients. Bring to a boil, then simmer 40 minutes. Strain and discard solids. Serve hot or cold. Flaxseed is a good optional topping.

CANYON RANCH MISO SOUP FOR 4

1/3 cup finely minced shallots
½ Tbsp. sesame oil
2 Tbsp. miso paste
1 quart vegetable stock
¼ cup diced firm tofu
2 Tbsp. sliced scallions

In medium saucepan over medium heat, sauté shallots in oil until translucent. Add miso paste. Stir well. Add stock. Bring to a simmer. Reduce heat to low for 10–15 minutes. Garnish with tofu and scallions.

Note: Miso loses nutritional qualities when allowed to boil. Always simmer miso over low heat.

EASY PEA SOUP

Recipe makes 2–4 servings.

2 scallions, finely sliced
1 minced clove garlic
1 Tbsp. garlic-infused oil
2 10-oz. packages frozen peas
3 cups chicken broth
2–3 Tbsp. grated Parmesan cheese

In a saucepan over medium-low heat, cook scallions in the oil. Stir until warm, then add frozen peas. Stir well with a wooden spoon. Add broth.

Cover and cook until peas are tender, about 5–10 minutes. Remove from heat and allow to cool.

Transfer soup to blender. Add cheese and purée until smooth. Serve immediately or reheat to taste.

NOTES AND VARIATIONS

SIDE DISHES

VEGETABLE ADVICE

EVERY VEGETABLE: Cook every vegetable until crispy-tender. If it's canned, heat gently. Salt and pepper and butter, taste and serve. And you can always add a dash of Lawry's® Seasoned Salt.

ASPARAGUS: Try a fleck of nutmeg, sea salt, a few capers or snipped chives, chervil, or slivered almonds. Good Seasons® Italian Dressing, tarragon vinegar, Parmesan cheese, or eggs— fried or hardboiled—are other tasty options.

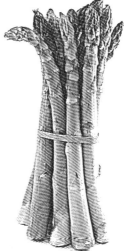

BEETS: To zip them up, add sautéed minced onion, tarragon vinegar, and lemon juice. Or add grated orange rind, snipped dill or tarragon, caraway seeds, a bit of prepared mustard, a dash of cloves, or allspice. Great topped with sour cream mixed with horseradish.

BROCCOLI: Enhance flavor with poppy seeds, sautéed mushrooms, curry, garlic, sautéed minced onions, tarragon, or marjoram.

BRUSSELS SPROUTS: Flavor with lemon juice, Parmesan, curry or tarragon vinegar, slivered almonds, sautéed mushrooms, caraway seeds, nutmeg, or sage.

CABBAGE: Flavor with curried butter, lemon juice, crisp bacon bits, caraway, dill, celery or poppy seeds, grated cheese, chili sauce, mustard, oregano, a dash of soy sauce, or slivers of garlic.

CARROTS: Sprinkle with chili or curry, poppy seeds, ginger, thyme, nutmeg, grated cheese, snipped mint, chervil, parsley, dill, or chives. Other options include crisp bacon or oregano.

CAULIFLOWER: Thinly sliced, it cooks faster and tastes elegant. Add slivered dill pickles, chili, prepared mustard, sour cream, chili sauce, or soy. Other options include cheese, slivered almonds, curry powder, mace, poppy seeds, ginger, dill, rosemary, basil, savory, or tarragon.

CORN: Off the cob, it takes kindly to minced onion or crisp bacon bits. On the cob, try adding chili, curry, garlic salt, mayonnaise, or celery seeds.

GREEN BEANS: Flavor with anchovy paste, slivered almonds, garlic, sautéed chopped mushrooms, or thin slices of sweet onions served on top. Also try finely diced bacon and onion sautéed together, along with 1 teaspoon prepared mustard or horseradish added to ¼ cup of butter. Another option is cooking with diced canned water chestnuts or herbs, including: oregano, rosemary, savory, dill, nutmeg, curry, chili sauce, or caraway seeds.

LIMAS: Add celery, garlic or onion salt, celery seeds, chili sauce, curry, basil, savory, or grated cheese. Another tasty option is cooking with sautéed mushrooms or scallions and a little mustard.

MUSHROOMS: Fresh or canned, mushrooms taste marvelous with minced onion, lemon juice, or a bit of sherry mixed with butter.

ONIONS: Apply any of the following to enhance the taste: cook small onions whole with sour cream. Slice and sauté big onions with generous amounts of pepper or a little sherry, chili, curry powder, caraway seeds, soy sauce, nutmeg, cloves, almonds, snipped parsley, or mint.

PEAS: Peas taste wonderful with sour cream, mayonnaise, curry powder, slivered almonds, chili, marjoram, or savory. A sprinkle of scallions, chives, mint, grated cheese, wine, cocktail onions, or diced canned water chestnuts are other delicious options.

POTATOES: If they're mashed, try adding grated cheese, sour cream with horseradish, or garlic. Boiled or baked: top with caraway, poppy, sesame seeds, rosemary, mint, dill, or crumbled blue cheese.

SPINACH AND OTHER GREENS: Consider adding nutmeg, rosemary, slivered almonds, poppy or sesame seeds, chili sauce, sour cream with horseradish, French dressing, bacon bits, lemon juice, wine, cayenne, garlic, or a shake of Worcestershire sauce.

SWEET POTATOES: Topped with cinnamon, cloves, nutmeg, or mace—it works magic. Adding sautéed walnuts, canned crushed pineapple, a spoonful of sherry, or 2 spoonfuls of orange juice sprinkled on top enhances the sweet flavor.

ACORN SQUASH: This vegetable tastes appealing with Parmesan cheese, minced onion, brown sugar and sherry, honey, orange juice, and a sprinkle nutmeg. Or add canned small onions with walnuts and pour a combination of light molasses, melted butter, cinnamon, salt, and pepper over the top and bake for 45 minutes.

SUMMER SQUASH: Tastes great with grated cheese, soy sauce, onion, sour cream with dill, oregano, nutmeg, chili sauce, bacon, chopped chives, scallions, parsley, or slivered tomatoes.

TOMATOES: This vegetable needs a lot of seasoning, so go heavy on salt, seasoned salt, and pepper. Add Roquefort, chili, or Worcestershire sauce for zest. Also try thyme, rosemary, basil, dill, oregano, sage, or marjoram.

ZUCCHINI: Try a dash of soy sauce, chili sauce, grated cheese, minced onion, marjoram, or basil to enhance the flavor.

WAYS TO COOK AN ARTICHOKE

TO BOIL:

Bring 3 inches of water to a boil. Stand prepared artichokes in saucepan. Cover and boil for 25–40 minutes or until center pulls out easily.

TO STEAM:

Place prepared artichokes on a rack above boiling water. Cover and steam for 25–40 minutes or until center pulls out easily.

TO MICROWAVE:

Place artichoke upside down in a glass bowl with ¼ cup water, ½ Tbsp. lemon juice, and ½ Tbsp. olive oil. Cover bowl and cook on high for 7 minutes.

SAUCES

GARLIC/MAYO	LEMON-THYME	HOLLANDAISE
Mix:	Whisk:	Mix in blender:
3/4 cup low-fat mayo	1 stick butter, melted	2 large egg yolks
1 to 2 cloves garlic, mashed	1 tsp. dried thyme	1 tsp. warm water
Salt	1 tsp. lemon juice	1 tsp. lemon juice
Pepper	3/4 tsp. coarse salt	1 stick butter
Serve cold.	Serve hot or cooled.	Serve hot or cooled.

JULIE'S ARTICHOKE SURPRISE FOR 4

1 cup uncooked rice
1 11½-oz. can chicken broth
2 6-oz. jars marinated artichoke hearts, save juice
¼ tsp. curry powder
1/3 cup mayo
4 green onions, chopped
½ green pepper, chopped

Preheat oven to 350 degrees.

Cook rice in broth and enough water to make 2 cups liquid. Take juice from artichokes and combine in a bowl with mayo and curry. Stir onion, peppers, and artichokes into rice. Stir, adding mayo and curry mixture. Cover and bake for 20 minutes. Add cooked chicken to make a heartier dish.

ARTICHOKE HEARTS WITH RED PEPPERS & ONIONS

1 Tbsp. EVOO
1 garlic clove, minced
1 small sweet onion, sliced
1 large sweet red pepper cut in 1 ½-inch pieces
1 can water-packed artichoke hearts, drained and cut in half

In EVOO, gently sauté garlic, onions, and red peppers until soft. Add artichokes and cook over low heat until blended. Let sit, then heat again. Tastes better the next day.

ASPARAGUS

Asparagus
Cherry tomatoes
Anchovies
Garlic clove
EVOO
Red pepper flakes
Good Seasons® Italian dressing with Balsamic
vinegar

Stir-fry asparagus with cut-up cherry tomatoes, chopped anchovies, and thinly sliced garlic clove in olive oil. Add red pepper flakes to taste. Cook until asparagus bends slightly.

Add dressing. Good hot or cold.

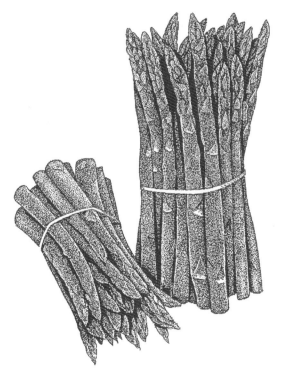

Optional Recipe:
   3 Tbsp. butter
   2 cups oyster mushrooms
   Sea salt
   Pepper
   1 lb. asparagus
   3 scallions
   1 Tbsp. butter
   ½ cup frozen peas
   1 tsp. tarragon

In a large skillet over medium heat, melt 2 Tbsp. butter. Add oyster mushrooms or other mushrooms cut into 3/4" pieces. Add sea salt and pepper. Cook 5 minutes. Stir in 1" pieces of asparagus, thinly sliced scallions, and butter. Add salt and pepper. Cover and cook 2 minutes for thin asparagus, or 7 minutes for fat asparagus, until al dente.

Stir in frozen peas and tarragon. Cover and cook until asparagus is tender.

CRISP GARDEN VEGETABLES FOR 8

16 tiny new potatoes
8 small zucchinis
4 small turnips, peeled and quartered
16 baby carrots
8 baby leeks
3 red peppers, cut bite-sized
¼ cup melted butter
Parmesan cheese
Paprika

Microwave vegetable medley in bunches 3–4 minutes. Put in Pyrex dish and drizzle ¼ cup melted butter over the vegetables. Toss to coat. Season to taste. Cover with grated Parmesan and a sprinkle of paprika.

Roast vegetables for about 30 minutes or until tender. Quantity can be adjusted to the size of the crowd.

ANDREA'S ROASTED VEGETABLES

3 Tbsp. olive oil
¼ cup shredded basil
2 garlic bulbs, separated into cloves and peeled
1 tsp. Tony Chachere's® Creole seasoning
1 zucchini, cut into ½" rounds
1 small eggplant, cut in large pieces
4 plum Italian tomatoes, quartered
1 each medium red and yellow peppers, cut
1 large purple onion

Preheat oven to 450 degrees.

Toss all ingredients together in a large roasting pan. Bake for 30–40 minutes, stirring every ten minutes.

Note: Add other vegetables for variety.

JACKIE'S BLACK-EYED PEAS

    1 11-oz. pkg. fresh black-eyed peas
    1 cup chicken stock
    1 cup water
    8 oz. bacon, cut into pieces and fried
    1/8 tsp. pepper
    1 Tbsp. soy sauce
    1 Tbsp. catsup

Combine all ingredients and bring to boil. Simmer 30 minutes, then serve.

PAUL HOCHULI'S BLACK-EYED PEAS*

    1 lb. fresh black-eyed peas
    ½ tsp. black pepper
    Pinch red pepper
    Pinch dry horseradish
    Pinch chili powder
    2 small onions, quartered
    Dash Tabasco®
    2 cloves garlic, chopped
    Dash Worcestershire sauce
    2 slices bacon, cut into pieces
    Half as much beer as water

Rinse off peas. In a large bowl, mix black and red pepper, dry horseradish, chili powder, quartered onions, Tabasco®, garlic, Worcestershire sauce, and raw bacon slices. Soak peas and other ingredients overnight in beer and water.

Cook slowly in pan, adding beer as liquid boils away.

* This recipe is to YOUR taste. Some like 'em hotter than others. Taste often.

GOOD LUCK BLACK-EYED PEAS

Makes 8–10 servings.

    4 15-oz. cans black-eyed peas
    2 jalapeños (canned), seeded, and finely chopped
    1 large onion, chopped fine
    Bacon

Combine ingredients in 2-qt. saucepan and simmer
slowly until most of the liquid evaporates, about 1 to 1
½ hours. Cook bacon, and sauté onion in bacon fat, if
desired. Add to mixture. Serve.

HOPPIN' JOHN FOR 4

    1 pkg. black-eyed peas
    1/3 lb. bacon
    1 large onion, sliced
    1 sprig celery leaves
    2 cups water
    ½ cup rice
    Chopped parsley

Cook fresh black-eyed peas by pkg. directions. Cut bacon in squares. Brown in hot
skillet. Sauté onion and celery leaves. Add to peas. Add water and rice. Simmer,
covered, until rice is fully cooked. Add more water if necessary. Top with chopped
parsley.

BRAISED BELGIAN ENDIVES FOR 4

8 endives, about 1 ½ lb.
1 Tbsp. butter
Juice of ½ lemon
½ cup water
1 Tbsp. sugar
Salt
Pepper

Trim off darkened ends on each endive. Arrange in one layer in a heavy skillet. Add butter, lemon juice, water, sugar, salt, and pepper; cover. Bring to boil and simmer 25 minutes.

BAKED ENDIVES WITH PARMESAN CHEESE

8 cooked, well-drained endives
2 Tbsp. butter
¼ cup freshly grated Parmesan

Preheat oven to 425 degrees.

Butter bottom of a baking dish. Add endives. Sprinkle with cheese and dot with remaining butter. Bake for 15 min. Remove from oven and place in broiler until browned and nicely glazed.

BROCCOLI & CAULIFLOWER

Recipe serves 10.

3 Tbsp. olive oil
1 large red bell pepper, cut into thin strips
3 garlic cloves, minced
6 cups broccoli flowerets
6 cups cauliflower flowerets
¼ cup drained capers

Heat oil in a 12-inch skillet. Sauté pepper until tender. Add garlic. Sauté 30 seconds longer. Add broccoli, cauliflower, capers, and water. Cover and steam about 5 minutes. Serve hot.

BRUSSELS SPROUTS WITH LEMON

2 lbs. Brussels sprouts, bottoms cut off, halved, and thinly sliced
2 Tbsp. freshly squeezed lemon juice
2 Tbsp. butter
3 garlic cloves, minced
2 tsp. poppy seeds
2 Tbsp. olive oil
¼ cup white wine or vermouth

Grated zest of one lemon

Transfer sprouts to bowl with lemon juice. Refrigerate, covered, for up to 3 hours.

When ready to serve, add sprouts, butter, garlic, and poppy seeds to hot oil in skillet. Add wine and stir, then add 3/4 lemon zest. Sprinkle rest of zest on top, then serve.

SUZY'S MICROWAVE CAULIFLOWER

1 head cauliflower, cored and rinsed
¾ cup mayo
1 Tbsp. mustard
Jarlsberg cheese, grated

Take 1 head of cauliflower. Place head up in a bowl with a small bit of water in the bottom. Cover and microwave 6–7 minutes.

"Frost" with mixture of mayo and mustard. Sprinkle with grated Jarlsberg. Microwave until cheese melts.

RED CABBAGE FOR 4

6 cups finely shredded red cabbage
4 slices chopped bacon
4 Tbsp. onion, finely chopped
4 Tbsp. brown sugar
3 Tbsp. vinegar or white wine
1 tsp. caraway seeds

Cook cabbage over low heat. Add chopped bacon, then add finely chopped onion, brown sugar, vinegar or white wine, and caraway seeds.

Place cabbage in pan, cover, and simmer until tender.

Canned red cabbage may be substituted. Drain. Rinse. Mix with above until hot, about 5 minutes.

GREEN CABBAGE FOR 4

1 head of cabbage, sliced thin
2 small Granny Smith apples, chopped
¼ cup balsamic vinegar
¼ cup EVOO
Salt
Pepper

Place apples and cabbage in pan with water.
Drizzle balsamic vinegar and olive oil on top.
Stir until done. Salt and pepper for taste.

JACK'S CABBAGE FOR 2

½ head cabbage, sliced
2 cloves garlic, sliced
2 Tbsp. olive oil
½ cup chicken broth
Salt
Pinch red pepper flakes

Sauté cabbage and garlic in olive oil. Add chicken broth to steam.

Season with salt and red pepper flakes to taste.

MORE CABBAGE THOUGHTS

2 onions, halved and thinly sliced
½ head cabbage
1 tsp. caraway
2 tsp. sesame seeds
6 Tbsp. EVOO
2 tsp. salt
2 pinches cayenne
2 Tbsp. lemon juice

Mix onions, cabbage, caraway, and sesame seeds in olive oil. Place in skillet. Cook ½ of mixture over medium heat until golden. Remove from heat. Just before serving add salt and cayenne; continue cooking for about 7 minutes. Add lemon juice, then serve.

CARROTS LYONNAISE

6 cups carrots, chopped
3 Tbsp. butter
1 large yellow onion, chopped
Thyme
1/3 cup sugar
1 tsp. salt
1 tsp. pepper

Note: All of the above ingredients should be in proportion to amount of carrots.

Sauté all ingredients in butter. Add carrots chopped ¼ inch thick.
Cover and cook over low heat.

YUMMY BAKED ONIONS

4 onions, peeled
¼ cup balsamic vinegar
¼ tsp. salt
1/8 tsp. pepper
1 Tbsp. butter, divided into 4 pats (one pat per onion)

Preheat oven to 325 degrees.

Cook 1 hour covered, then 30 minutes uncovered.

BAKED GARLIC

8 whole heads fresh garlic
2 Tbsp. butter
2 Tbsp. EVOO
2 tsp. rosemary or oregano

Preheat oven to 375 degrees.

Remove outer layers of skin from garlic, leaving cloves and head intact. Place on two sheets of foil. Top with butter, oil, and herbs. Fold up foil and seal.

Bake for 1 hour.

ROOT VEGETABLE GRATIN WITH GRUYÈRE

1 Tbsp. unsalted butter
3 garlic cloves, minced
3 cups heavy cream
Salt
Fresh-ground pepper
¼ tsp. freshly grated nutmeg
1 lb. parsnips
1 lb. sweet potatoes
1 lb. celery root, peeled and sliced 1/8" thick
8 oz. shredded Gruyère cheese
1 tsp. minced fresh thyme
3 tsp. minced flat parsley

Preheat oven 400.

Butter 3-qt baking dish. Over medium heat, melt butter. Add garlic. Cook 1 minute. Add cream and remaining ingredients. Heat until bubbles form, then let sit 10 minutes off heat.

Arrange layers of parsnips, then sweet potatoes, then celery root. Sprinkle half of cheese, repeat layer, until all ingredients are used up.

Cover dish with foil. Place on baking sheet and bake for 1 hour. Remove foil. Bake 15–30 minutes longer. Let stand 15 minutes before serving.

AUDREY'S BAKED LIMA BEAN CASSEROLE FOR 4–5

½ cup chopped onion
¼ cup chopped green pepper
¼ cup chopped celery
1 ½ Tbsp. vegetable oil
2 cans broad yellow lima beans
4 Tbsp. catsup
2 tsp. brown sugar
1 dash Tabasco

Preheat oven to 375 degrees.

Microwave onion, peppers, and celery in oil in a measuring cup for one minute, stirring once. Place all ingredients in a small, sprayed casserole dish. Bake for 30 minutes.

SPINACH MADELEINE

2 pkg. frozen spinach
4 Tbsp. butter
2 Tbsp. flour
2 Tbsp. chopped onion
½ cup spinach liquid
½ cup evaporated milk
½ tsp. pepper
3/4 tsp. celery salt
½ tsp. salt
1 Tbsp. Worcestershire sauce
1 6-oz. roll jalapeño cheese/Monterrey Jack

Preheat oven to 350 degrees.

Cook spinach. Set aside. Save liquid. Melt butter and blend in flour. Add onion and liquid; stir until thickened. Add seasoning and cut up cheese. Add spinach and bake for 20–25 minutes.

SICILIAN SPINACH

1 pkg. frozen spinach
1 Tbsp. EVOO
1 clove garlic, minced
4 chopped anchovies

Squeeze water from cooked spinach. Sauté in skillet with olive oil and minced clove garlic. Add chopped anchovies. Season to taste.

BAKED LEEKS

4 leeks
1 Tbsp. EVOO
1 clove garlic, minced
½ cup white wine
½ cup sour cream
Horseradish to taste

Preheat oven to 400 degrees.

Halve leeks. Rinse. Cover the bottom of a baking dish with one layer of leeks. Brush with EVOO. Sprinkle with minced garlic and season. Add white wine.

Bake covered for 15 minutes, then continue baking uncovered for 10 additional minutes.

Top with mixture of sour cream and horseradish.

GREEN BEANS, MUSTARD SAUCE & TOASTED ALMONDS

1 pkg. frozen pearl onions
4 Tbsp. butter
4 Tbsp. Dijon mustard
2 lbs. green beans cut into 2-inch pieces
3/4 cup chicken broth

In a large, deep skillet, sauté onions in 2 Tbsp. butter and Dijon until golden. Remove from heat.

Add green beans and broth. Cook. Sauté almonds in 2 Tbsp. butter until brown. Combine onions and beans. Heat.

Add almonds and season to taste.

CAMPBELL'S® SOUP GREEN BEAN CASSEROLE

8 cups cooked French cut green beans
2 2/3 cup French's French fried onions
2 cans cream of mushroom soup
2 tsp. soy sauce
1 cup milk
¼ tsp. ground black pepper

Preheat oven to 350 degrees.

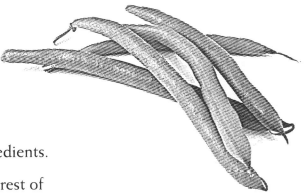

In a 3-qt casserole dish, mix beans and 1 1/3 cup onions with rest of the ingredients.

Bake for 25 minutes. Stir the mix, add the rest of the onions, and bake for an additional 5 minutes.

RATATOUILLE

Recipe serves 8–10.

   5 Tbsp. EVOO
   2 Tbsp. bacon grease
   1 large yellow onion, diced
   3 cloves garlic
   1 large red bell pepper, diced
   6 medium zucchini, diced (each round into 4)
   1 medium eggplant, diced with skin on
   4–6 medium tomatoes, peeled and diced
   Grated Parmesan cheese

In 4 Tbsp. EVOO and 2 teaspoons of bacon grease, sauté onion and 2 cloves minced garlic. Add bell pepper and cook until soft. Add zucchini and cook until al dente. Add eggplant and cook until soft. Add tomatoes and all the juice. Add remaining clove of garlic, pressed.

Drizzle 1 Tbsp. remaining EVOO over ingredients. Cook over very low heat. Salt and pepper to taste.

Serve warm with a sprinkle of Parmesan.

Note: Tastes better if you prepare day before and reheat.

SUMMER SQUASH SAUTÉ

Recipe makes 8 cups.

    4 medium zucchini
    4 medium yellow squash
    1 ¼ oz. taco seasoning mix
    ¼ tsp. cayenne
    1 Tbsp. vegetable oil
    4 medium tomatoes
    2 medium onions

Slice squash into ¼-inch rounds. Place in large bowl. Sprinkle with taco seasoning plus cayenne. Toss until well coated. Heat oil in skillet, add squash, and sauté 5 minutes. Peel tomatoes and cut into quarters. Slice onions in ¼-inch slices, then divide into rings. Sauté 5 more minutes.

Drain before serving.

HOW TO COOK CORN ON THE COB

Fill a large kettle with cold water and bring to a rolling boil. Add the corn and immediately turn off the heat. Allow to stand for 5 minutes and remove the exact number of ears you need for each person. Keep the pot uncovered and remove the rest of the ears as needed.

Alternative Method:

Place corn in boiling water. Cover. When water returns to boil, remove from heat and let stand 5–20 minutes.

CORN WITH CHILIES & CHEESE

Recipe serves 12.

1 large white onion, chopped
3 4-oz. cans peeled green chilies
3–4 Tbsp. EVOO
6 cups corn or 4 large cans corn, not creamed
12 oz. Monterrey Jack jalapeño cheese, grated
Salt
Pepper

Sauté onions and chilies 5 minutes in olive oil. Add corn and cook until heated through. Fold cheese into mixture, letting it melt.

Salt and pepper to taste.

Can be microwaved to reconstitute.

CORN PUDDING

1 cup milk
4 eggs
2 Tbsp. flour
½ tsp. salt
2 tsp. sugar
¼ cup butter
Dash of pepper
1 can creamed corn

Preheat oven to 350 degrees.

In a blender, mix the milk, eggs, flour, salt, sugar, and butter. Blend until butter is homogenized. Season with pepper. Pour into a casserole dish. Stir in a can of creamed corn and bake for 1 hour.

MASEY'S CORN SOUFFLÉ FOR 10–12

2 boxes Jiffy® corn muffin mix
2 regular cans creamed corn
2 8-oz. containers sour cream
2 eggs
1 bunch green onions, chopped
To add a little kick: 2 finely chopped seeded and deveined jalapeño peppers.

Preheat oven to 350 degrees.

Whisk above ingredients and place in a greased casserole dish. Bake for 1 to 1 ½ hours until done or toothpick comes out clean.

CORN CASSEROLE

4 oz. cream cheese
¼ cup milk
2 Tbsp. butter
1 4.5-oz. can chopped green chili peppers
2 cans of white "shoe peg" corn, drained

In a microwave, melt cream cheese, milk, butter, and peppers. Place corn in a baking dish and cover with the mix. Bake covered for 30 minutes.

Remove cover and cook for 15–20 minutes longer.

TIP ON COOKING PASTA

Do not add oil to the boiling water because the oil coats the pasta and doesn't allow the sauce to adhere.

CORRINE'S NOODLES FOR 12

12–16 oz. egg noodles
16 oz. sour cream
1 pint cottage cheese, small curd
2 Tbsp. Worcestershire sauce
2 dashes Tabasco
1 clove garlic, crushed
4 tsp. grated onion
2 tsp. poppy seeds
Parmesan or Longhorn cheese, grated

Preheat oven to 350 degrees.

Cook noodles until not quite done. Combine remaining ingredients. Add cooked noodles in a buttered casserole. Top with Parmesan or grated Longhorn cheese just before cooking. Can top with toasted almonds after cooking.

Bake for 30 minutes.

WILD RICE

Basic preparation: For each cup rinsed rice use 4 cup salted water.

Bring to boil. Cover and simmer 45 minutes, or until tender.

Optional additions:
    1 large chopped onion
    1 lb. chopped mushrooms sautéed in butter
    Sautéed garlic

TEXMATI® RICE

1 cup Texmati® rice
2 cups water
1 Tbsp. butter
Salt

Put all ingredients in pot and bring to boil. Stir once, cover tightly, then simmer 15 minutes. Remove from heat. Let stand covered 10 minutes before serving.

NUTTED WILD RICE FOR 6

1 cup raw wild rice
5 ½ cup de-fatted chicken stock
1 cup shelled pecan halves
1 cup yellow raisins
Grated rind of one large orange
3 tsp. dried mint

4 green onions, thinly sliced
¼ cup EVOO
1/3 cup fresh orange juice
1 ½ tsp. salt
Fresh ground pepper

Rinse rice. Place in pan and add stock (or water). Bring to boil, then simmer uncovered for 45 minutes. After 30 minutes check for doneness; al dente is preferred. Drain rice. Put in bowl. Add remaining ingredients to rice and toss. Adjust seasons to taste. Let mix stand for at least 2 hours.

JACKIE'S BAKED SPICY RICE

Recipe serves 8.

2 Tbsp. vegetable oil
1 cup Texmati® rice
2 cans Rotel® tomatoes
1 cup water
1 tsp. salt
½ cup chopped onion
1 cup shredded Monterey Jack

Preheat oven to 350 degrees.

Heat oil in skillet. Add rice; brown. Transfer to a 2-qt. baking dish. Add tomatoes, water, salt, onion, and cheese. Stir. Cover. Bake 45 minutes. Uncover and stir. Bake additional 15 minutes.

ANDREA'S MEXICAN RICE FOR 8–10

8 pieces bacon, fried
2 cups rice
1 small yellow onion, chopped
2 cloves garlic, minced
2 cans chopped tomatoes
½ tsp. cumin
1 tsp. salt
4 cups chicken broth (2 cans + water to make up difference)

In a skillet, brown rice in bacon drippings for about 5 minutes, constantly stirring. Add remaining ingredients. Stir once and cover skillet.

Simmer 30 minutes, stirring from time to time. Allow rice to cool for 15 minutes before serving.

PINTO BEANS MELANIE

1 pkg. pinto beans, sorted and soaked
1 can beer
1 hunk salt pork
Garlic beads, smashed

In fresh water, bring beans to a boil. Add beer and pork. Cook slowly for several hours or until beans are tender, then serve.

BLACK BEANS RECIPE

1 large onion, chopped
3–4 cloves garlic, pressed
2 Tbsp. EVOO
1 pkg. black beans, soaked
1 bay leaf
3–4 Tbsp. dry sherry
2 tsp. green chili salsa

Sauté onion and garlic in olive oil until tender. Add mixture to soaked beans and water and bring to rolling boil. Add remaining ingredients. Cover and simmer for 1 ½ hours or until tender.

FAKE BAKED BEANS FOR 4

¼ cup catsup
¼ cup molasses
3 Tbsp. cider vinegar
1 ½ tsp. dry mustard powder
¼ tsp. freshly ground black pepper
¼ Tbsp. Tabasco® sauce
3 15-oz. cans of white beans, in their liquid
6 slices thick-cut bacon

Mix all ingredients but bacon and beans. Pour mixture into beans. Stir well. Add 1 slice of bacon. Let simmer 30–45 minutes. Fry remaining bacon. Drain and chop bacon.

Top beans with bacon. Add chopped red onion for additional flavor.

TED'S MICROWAVE ACORN SQUASH

1 medium acorn squash
1 Tbsp. butter
1/8 tsp. salt
Paprika
1 tsp. brown sugar
1 tsp. cream sherry

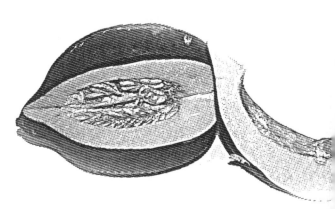

Cut acorn squash in half. Remove seeds. Place scooped side down in a glass dish with the bottom covered with ¼-inch water. Microwave on high for 7 minutes.

Turn over. Add butter, salt, a sprinkle of paprika, brown sugar, and cream sherry. Microwave uncovered for 3–5 more minutes.

Then bake in the oven at 375 degrees for 45 minutes or until tender.

BUD'S BUTTERNUT SQUASH

3 squash
½ cup half & half
½ cup light brown sugar
Butter

Preheat oven at 375 degrees.

Bake squash for 1 hour and 15 minutes. Seed, then scoop into a large pot. Mash until smooth. Add half & half and light brown sugar. Pour into square baking dish. Sprinkle brown sugar on top. Dot liberally with butter.

Bake again at 350 degrees for 30 minutes. Cool in refrigerator for 1 hour before serving.

JULIE'S ZUCCHINI QUICHE

3 cups diced zucchini
4 eggs
½ cup Parmesan cheese
1 tsp. marjoram
1 tsp. parsley
Onion slices

Preheat oven at 350 degrees.

Lay diced zucchini in baking dish. Mix eggs, cheese, marjoram, and parsley and pour over zucchini. Sprinkle onion slices on top.

Bake for 30 minutes.

CRUSTLESS QUICHE FOR 4

1 cup cream or half & half
3 eggs
¾ cup grated Swiss, Gruyere, or Cheddar cheese
¼ cup grated Parmesan
½ tsp. salt
¼ tsp. cayenne

Set rack in middle and preheat oven to 325 degrees.

Combine cream heated until warm, eggs at room temperature, grated cheeses, salt, and cayenne. Beat until well blended.

Pour mixture into 4–6 buttered ramekins or pie plate and bake 20–30 minutes until almost firm. Cool on rack. Serve at room temperature.

QUICK 'N EASY TOMATO PIE

1 9-inch frozen pie crust
2 tsp. Dijon mustard
1 Tbsp. olive oil
½ cup grated Swiss cheese
4–6 Roma tomatoes, cut into ¼-inch slices
Salt
Ground pepper

Preheat oven to 350 degrees.

Spread mustard on bottom of the pie crust. Spread olive oil over mustard. Next sprinkle a layer of cheese. Top with layer of tomatoes. Season and bake 30 minutes or until crust is golden brown.

VIRGINIA'S TOMATO PIE

1 pre-baked deep dish pie shell
2 small red onions, sliced thin
1 small bunch fresh basil, chopped
3–4 ripe tomatoes, sliced
Black pepper as needed
1 ½ cups mayonnaise
½ cup grated mozzarella
½ cup grated asiago

Preheat oven to 350 degrees.

Place sliced onion on bottom of the pie shell. Top with ½ the basil, adding 2 layers of tomatoes. Sprinkle with black pepper. Add remaining basil.

Layer rest of the tomatoes until the pie shell is full. Mix mayonnaise and both cheeses together. Spread over the top

Bake until top is lightly browned, 15–25 minutes. Let cool, then cut. May be served hot or cold.

CLAIRE'S RED PEPPERS STUFFED WITH TOMATOES & MOZZARELLA

    3 red bell peppers
    1 ½ Tbsp. EVOO
    1 ½ Tbsp. balsamic vinegar
    1 clove garlic, minced
    3/4 lb. cherry or Roma tomatoes, cut in ½-inch bites.
    1 cup cubed mozzarella
    ½ cup basil leaves, cut into thin strips

Preheat oven to 375 degrees.

Bake peppers 40 minutes, or until tender.

Take red bell peppers and halve them lengthwise. Cut a thin slice from the rounded side so that each will sit upright in a pan.

In a large bowl, whisk remaining ingredients. Fill each pepper with the mixture and bake until mozzarella melts.

SAUTÉED OKRA

    1 lb. small okra
    2 Tbsp. olive oil
    Red pepper flakes

Trim stems off okra, being careful not to cut into the pods. Pour oil into a large skillet over medium-high heat. Add okra and red pepper flakes. Sauté until pods have softened slightly, about 6–7 minutes. Season to taste.

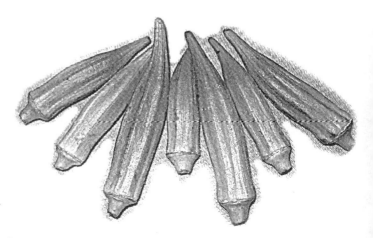

DEEP FRIED OKRA FOR 6

1 large egg
1/3 cup milk
2 cups dry bread crumbs (or corn meal)
3 cups corn oil
1 lb. okra, rinsed and cut into ½-inch pieces

In a large bowl, whisk together egg and milk. Put bread crumbs or corn meal in a second bowl

Heat oil in a heavy 12-inch skillet on medium-high heat until oil is hot enough to toast a bread crumb in 30 seconds. Toss half the okra in egg mix until coated. Let excess drip into bowl. Transfer to bread crumb/corn meal mix and coat.

Add okra to hot oil and cook until well-browned, about 5 minutes. Remove and drain on paper.

Repeat with second batch and season with salt and pepper. Serve hot.

BAKED POTATOES

Use Idaho baking potatoes, up to one pound each.

Preheat oven to 475 degrees.

Scrub and prick each potato twice. Bake uncovered on the middle rack for 1 hour. Can store in Ziploc® bag for up to 3 days in refrigerator.

SMALL POTATOES WITH GARLIC & ROSEMARY

New or salt potatoes
Garlic cloves, pressed
Rosemary
Butter
Salt
Pepper

Preheat oven to 350 degrees.

Cut potatoes. Mix remaining ingredients into paste. Toss potatoes in paste, then place in pan or dish so they don't stick. Bake for 45 minutes, then bake 10–15 minutes longer at 350 degrees. Cool before serving.

CONNIE'S WONDERFUL POTATOES

6 baking potatoes
Pam® olive oil spray
Rosemary
Salt
Pepper

Preheat oven to 450 degrees.

Cut baking potatoes in half lengthwise, then cut into narrow slices. Put them slanted into rectangular glass baking dish. Sprinkle with rosemary, then spray liberally with Pam® olive oil. Salt and pepper to taste. Let sit 2 hours, then re-spray with Pam® before baking.

Bake for 45 minutes to 1 hour.

ROASTED POTATOES

Potatoes
2 Tbsp. EVOO
Cloves garlic, unpeeled

Preheat oven to 400 degrees.

Cut potatoes into 1-inch squares, then place in roasting pan. Drizzle oil over them. Add a few unpeeled cloves of garlic. Roast at 400 degrees for 45 minutes, then reduce heat to 325 degrees for another 20 minutes.

NO-BRAIN ONION ROASTED POTATOES FOR 4

lb. new potatoes or 4 medium all-purpose potatoes
1/3 cup olive oil
1 pkg. Lipton® onion soup mix

Preheat oven to 425 degrees.

In 13x9 roasting pan, combine all ingredients until evenly coated. Bake uncovered, stirring occasionally, for 35 minutes or until potatoes are tender and golden brown.

Expand all ingredients until you have the right amount to serve your number of guests.

LEEK & GARLIC MASHED POTATOES FOR 8

3 leeks, cut into ½-inch pieces
1 Tbsp. minced garlic
1 tsp. canola oil
1 ½ lbs. russet potatoes, peeled and quartered
1 bay leaf
1 tsp. kosher salt
¼ tsp. fresh ground pepper
Skim milk
½ cup non-fat plain yogurt

Sauté leeks and garlic for 3–4 minutes in oil. Add potatoes, bay leaf, salt, and pepper. Add water to cover vegetables. Bring to boil. Simmer covered for 10 minutes. Uncover and simmer 10–15 minutes longer. Drain. Discard bay leaf.

Using a mixer, beat until smooth. Gradually add skim milk until creamy. Add yogurt for creamier texture.

COTTAGE POTATOES FOR 4

3 large Idaho potatoes
½ stick butter
1 cup cottage cheese
½ onion, diced
Salt
Pepper
Paprika

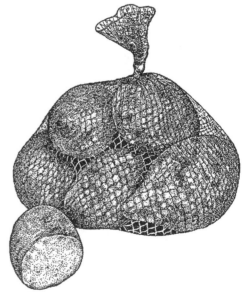

Preheat oven to 350 degrees.

Scrub and slice potatoes. Boil until tender. Drain and mash with 2 Tbsp. butter. Add cottage cheese, onion, and season to taste. Put in greased casserole dish. Dot with remaining butter and sprinkle with paprika.

Bake uncovered for 30 minutes.

SUPERIOR POTATO CASSEROLE

1 pkg. frozen Ore-Ida® hash browns with onions and peppers
1 8-oz. cream cheese
1 stick melted butter
1 can cream of chicken soup
1 cup shredded cheddar

Preheat oven to 350 degrees.

Butter a 9x13 glass bakeware dish. Defrost hash browns. Mix remaining ingredients and pour over hash browns.

Bake covered for 40–45 minutes. Then bake uncovered 10–15 minutes or until browned.

YUMMY GOOD EASY POTATOES

1 potato per person
1 onion for 4 potatoes
Salt
Pepper
Oregano
Shortening

Preheat oven to 300 degrees.

Peel thin-skinned potatoes and grate onion.

Grease doubled heavy foil with shortening. Add one layer of potatoes, salt, pepper, and onion. Sprinkle with oregano. Repeat for the second layer. Dot each layer with shortening. Roll up foil and seal.

Cook for 1 hour.

SWEET POTATOES FOR 6

4 medium sweet potatoes
Butter
1 head roasted garlic
½ cup milk
1 bunch green onions

Preheat oven to 350 degrees.

Butter potato skins and bake until skin crispy. After cooked, scoop out potato meat. Mash one head of roasted garlic and add dab of butter and hot milk to mixture. Add one whole bunch of green onions cut up (both tops and bottoms) and sautéed. Add mix to bottoms and bake 1 hour or until tender.

CUT-UP SWEET POTATOES FOR 6

2 lbs. sweet potatoes, cut in 1-inch chunks
2 medium Vidalia or sweet onions in 1-inch chunks
3 Tbsp. olive oil
¼ cup amaretto liqueur
1 tsp. dried thyme
Salt
Fresh ground pepper
¼ cup sliced almonds, toasted

Preheat oven to 425 degrees.

Toss all ingredients but the almonds in a shallow baking dish. Cover and bake 30 minutes. Then uncover and bake 20 minutes longer. Sprinkle with almonds before serving.

SCALLOPED SWEET POTATO AND APPLE FOR 8

2 lbs. potatoes, peeled and thinly sliced
1 Granny Smith apple—peeled, cored, and thinly sliced
12 dried apricot halves, chopped
3/4 cup honey
2 Tbsp. frozen orange juice concentrate
½ cup apple cider
½ tsp. salt
Ground pepper

Preheat oven to 370 degrees.

Spray 8-inch square baking dish with Pam® cooking oil spray. Line bottom layer with ½ of the potatoes, overlapping. Line second layer with all of the apple, overlapping. Line third layer of potatoes, overlapping. Sprinkle with chopped apricots.

Whisk together honey, frozen orange juice concentrate, apple cider, salt, and ground pepper. Pour honey mix over potatoes.

Cover with foil and bake for 40 minutes. Uncover and bake 15 minutes longer or until potatoes are tender.

FRESH CRANBERRY SAUCE 1

1 cup water
2 cups sugar
1 pkg. fresh cranberries

Place in a saucepan water and sugar. Stir until sugar dissolves. Boil syrup for 5 minutes.

Add fresh cranberries, washed and sorted. Gently cook uncovered for 3–5 minutes without stirring, until the skins pop. Skim, then chill.

FRESH CRANBERRY SAUCE 2

12 oz. cranberries
1 large orange
½ cup sugar
Water

Wash and sort berries. Grate orange rind. Squeeze orange into cup and add water to make 1 full cup. Mix everything together and let stand 5 minutes. Cook 5 minutes. Let stand off heat 5 minutes. Cook 10 minutes more.

Some suggest not letting all the berries pop.

FRESH CRANBERRY SAUCE VARIATIONS

Add 1 cup apple juice to above recipe.

SPIKED

Add to above recipe:
1 cup orange juice
6 Tbsp. Grand Marnier

BAKED CHUTNEYED PEACHES

1 large can peach halves (or 2 peach halves per person)
1 Tbsp. Major Grey's chutney

Preheat oven to 350 degrees.

Spoon chutney in center of peach half. Bake for 20–30 minutes.

NOTES AND VARIATIONS

ENTREES

ADIRONDACK TROUT GRANDMA BETSY

1 or more fish
Cooking oil
For each fish, use:
1 onion, sliced
1 lemon, sliced
2 Tbsp. Worcestershire sauce
2 tsp. Lawry's® Seasoned Salt

Preheat oven to 350 degrees.

Line baking pan with aluminum foil, then coat with a film of oil. Slice onions and lemons. Slice open fish, then douse fish with Worcestershire sauce. Sprinkle seasoned salt inside and out. Stuff cavity with onions and lemons.

Bake until fully cooked. BUT do NOT overcook.

DRUNKEN SCALLOPS FOR 2

1 lb. scallops
1 ½ bunches green onions
1 box small mushrooms
1 box cherry tomatoes
Pam® Spray
2 Tbsp. butter
½ cup sherry

Rinse and drain scallops. If they are large, cut into bite-sized pieces. Place scallops in baggie with sherry. Slice green onions and mushrooms. Slice small cherry tomatoes to same quantity as onions and mushrooms.

Spray skillet with Pam® first, then melt butter. Sauté onions, mushrooms, and tomatoes. Add scallops; add sherry to taste.

Do not overcook. Add salt and pepper to taste. Recipe may be easily expanded.

CLASSIC SHRIMP SCAMPI FOR 4

1 3/4 lbs. extra large shrimp, shelled
2 Tbsp. butter
2 tsp. EVOO
4 garlic cloves, minced
½ cup white wine
Sea salt
Pepper flakes to taste
1/3 cup chopped parsley
Juice of ½ lemon

In a large skillet, melt butter and EVOO. Add garlic. Sauté 1 minute. Add wine and seasonings. Simmer 2 additional minutes.

Add shrimp. Sauté until just pink. Add lemon and parsley.

Serve over pasta or with crusty bread.

SCALLOPS WITH CAPERS FOR 4

1 ½ lbs. sea scallops
3/4 cups flour
3 tsp. vegetable oil
4 Tbsp. butter
½ cup drained capers
1 Tbsp. red wine vinegar
2 tsp. parsley, chopped

Coat scallops with flour and shake off excess. Heat oil and add a few scallops at a time without overcrowding the skillet. Turn each batch until they brown evenly all over. Set aside on a warm platter until all are done. Add oil as needed.

Wipe out skillet. Add butter. Add capers, shaking the skillet until the liquid from the capers evaporates. Stir in vinegar and pour the sauce over the scallops. Sprinkle with parsley and serve.

STIR-FRY SHRIMP FOR 2

20 shrimp, peeled and deveined
Soy sauce
4-6 thin slices of fresh ginger
1–2 beads garlic, sliced
Cooking oil
1 bunch green onions, cut on the slant
1 red pepper, cut
1 can sliced water chestnuts
1 cup broccoli florets
Chicken broth

Set aside shrimp in a dish with enough soy sauce to moisten.

In a deep pan or wok, sauté slices of fresh ginger and garlic in oil. Remove.

Add green onions, red pepper, water chestnuts, then broccoli. Add shrimp.

Add a little chicken broth and simmer until shrimp is fully cooked.

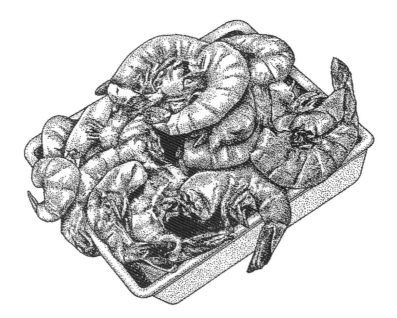

COQUILLE ST. JACQUES FOR 6

3 lbs. scallops
1 ½ pints white wine
Add a pinch of salt to the wine
6 Tbsp. butter
3 ½ cups mushrooms, sliced
6 green onions, sliced
2 tsp. minced parsley
Salt
Ground white pepper
Pinch marjoram
Pinch thyme
2 Tbsp. flour
4 tsp. heavy cream
Paprika
Fine breadcrumbs

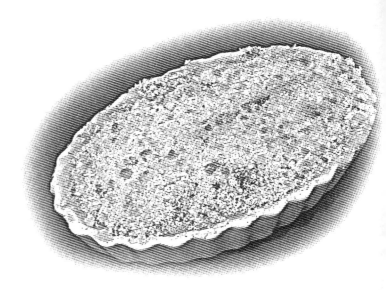

Simmer (do not boil) scallops in heated wine with salt until they become white, about 10 minutes. Set aside to keep warm. Reserve the liquid.

Melt butter in saucepan. Add mushrooms, chopped green onions, minced parsley, salt, ground pepper, marjoram, and thyme. When mushrooms and onions are tender, add flour and stir until smooth. Slowly add wine. Add enough rich cream to thicken the sauce. Add pinch of paprika and the scallops.

Cut each scallop into bite-sized pieces. Pour into a buttered casserole dish, then sprinkle with fine breadcrumbs. Dot with butter and cook until the crust is golden brown.

CRAB CASSEROLE FOR 12

3 cartons lump crab
3 cups soft bread, torn
3 cups Hellman's® mayo
1 ½ cups milk
9 hardboiled eggs, chopped
2 Tbsp. onions, chopped
½ cup lemon juice
Potato chips

Combine all ingredients but the potato chips and refrigerate.

Before cooking, top off mixture with crushed potato chips. Bake for 45 minutes at 350 degrees.

KISS CHICKEN GRANDMA BETSY

Chicken
Worcestershire sauce
Lawry's® Seasoned Salt

Preheat oven to 425 degrees.

Take chicken and quarter it or cut into single-serving pieces. Place skin side up in aluminum foil-lined pan. Douse with Worcestershire sauce. Sprinkle with seasoned salt.

Bake for 25–40 minutes, or until juices runs clear.

Note: You can do this with a whole 3 ½ lb chicken. Brush with oil. Season. Put in a shallow dish in oven at 450 degrees for 45 minutes. Remove and let stand covered for a few minutes to let the juices return to the center.

BAR B-Q CHICKEN

Preheat oven to 425 degrees.

Use any amount of quartered chicken; trim as much fat off as you can.

Pre-cook in oven for 20–30 minutes, then barbeque over low flame until done.

Sauce #1: Mix 1 part orange juice and 1 part Worcestershire sauce; baste until chicken is saturated.

Sauce #2: Use any commercial sauce, but I prefer Kraft's with onion bits.

NICOLE'S HAWAIIAN SHOSHEN CHICKEN

8–10 pieces chicken
Garlic
Onion salt
Pam® spray
Marinade:
1 cup water
½ cup soy sauce
½ cup sugar
½ tsp. fresh ginger
½ fresh diced garlic
1 tsp. sesame oil
1 bunch chopped green onions

Brown in Pam® 8–10 pieces dark chicken seasoned with garlic and onion salt to taste.

Mix marinade. Pour marinade over browned chicken. Sprinkle green onion on top. Cover and simmer 45 minutes, flipping every 15 minutes.

CORNISH GAME HEN

Cover 1 hen with Worcestershire sauce. Sprinkle with Lawry's® Seasoned Salt, and cook at 350 for one hour or until tender. Stuff cavity with lemons and garlic before cooking for additional flavor.

MM'S AMARETTO CHICKEN

Recipe serves 8–10.

    5 lbs. boned chicken breasts
    1 Tbsp. vegetable oil
    3 Tbsp. butter
    3 Tbsp. flour
    1 ½ tsp. salt
    1 ½ tsp. pepper,
    2 tsp. paprika
    1 ½ tsp. garlic salt
    1 ½ Tbsp. Dijon mustard
    1 6-oz. can oranges
    1 can water
    1 cup amaretto

Preheat oven to 350 degrees.

Sauté chicken in vegetable oil mixed with melted butter. Remove chicken from skillet and place in casserole dish.

Add to warm skillet Dijon mustard, oranges, water, and amaretto.

Stir over heat until thick. Pour sauce over chicken and bake 45 minutes.

JULIE'S EASY CHICKEN

Chicken breasts
1 can whole cranberries
1 bottle Wishbone® French dressing
1 pkg. Lipton® onion soup

Mix cranberries, French dressing, and Lipton onion soup. Pour over chicken breasts.

Bake for 35–45 minutes.

MICKEY'S VARIATION TO JULIE'S EASY CHICKEN

Pour 1 bottle Knott's Berry Farm® Sundried Tomato Vinaigrette over chicken breasts.

Bake at 350 for 35–45 minutes.

This is a tart and tangy alternative!

CHICKEN SAUTÉ

6 pieces chicken, preferably dark meat
Red wine vinegar
Olive oil
1 crushed garlic clove
Parsley
Dried tarragon
Salt
Pepper
10–12 whole mushrooms
Butter
Cooking sherry

Preheat oven to 325 degrees.

In a skillet, cook equal parts of red wine vinegar and olive oil, crushed clove of garlic, parsley, and dried tarragon. Add seasoned chicken, browning on both sides. Add mushrooms, cap down. Dot a little bit of butter on each mushroom.

Remove from skillet and place in oven for 25–30 minutes or until juices run clear when chicken pieces are pricked.

Remove from oven. Add sherry and deglaze pan until sauce thickens. Serve hot.

Note: Browning the chicken may be done earlier. Cover the skillet with aluminum foil and refrigerate. This way you can do a large amount of chicken for a big crowd.

BAKED MUSTARD-HERB CHICKEN LEGS

4 leg or thigh pieces chicken, cut in 2–8 legs or thighs
1 cup fresh bread crumbs
2 tsp. minced garlic
2 tsp. minced parsley
1 tsp. tarragon
Salt and pepper
4 Tbsp. Dijon mustard

Preheat oven to 425 degrees.

Combine bread crumbs, garlic, parsley, tarragon, and salt and pepper to taste on a plate. Use a pastry brush to paint mustard on chicken legs. Roll chicken in bread crumb mixture.

Place coated chicken in roasting pan and bake for 30–40 minutes.

COQ AU VIN FOR 6

4 lbs. chicken breasts and thighs
2 medium broilers, cut up
Salt
Pepper
Paprika
8 Tbsp. butter
½ lb. sliced fresh mushrooms or canned whole mushrooms
3 green onions, sliced
¼ tsp. thyme
¼ tsp. tarragon
1 bay leaf, crushed
1 large garlic clove, crushed
1 ½ cups red wine
¼ cup chicken broth
2 slices of bacon, fried crisp and crumbled
1 cup pearl onions, peeled or canned
1 tsp. minced parsley

Preheat oven to 325 degrees.

Brown seasoned chicken in 6 Tbsp. butter. After chicken is browned, remove and add remaining 2 Tbsp. butter to pan. Sauté mushrooms and green onions. Add thyme, tarragon, bay leaf, garlic, wine, and chicken broth. Simmer 5 minutes.

Place chicken in large shallow baking dish. Spoon wine mixture over chicken. Cover with foil and bake for 1 hour.

Add crumbled bacon and pearl onions. Cover again and bake 1 more hour.

Sprinkle with minced parsley before serving.

Serve with fluffy brown and white rice covered with sauce from chicken.

ONE VERSION OF BASQUE CHICKEN

6–8 pieces dark chicken
4 cloves garlic, peeled
2 Tbsp. EVOO
½ sliced onion
4 peeled chopped tomatoes
Wedges of green and red peppers
White wine

Brown chicken and garlic in 1 Tbsp. oil. Remove to one side. Add additional 1 Tbsp. oil. Add sliced onion, tomatoes, and green and red peppers. Add a little white wine.

Return chicken and garlic to pan. Steam, covered, for 20 minutes.

JACK'S POULET BASQUAISE

Chicken breasts
Salt
Pepper
2 Tbsp. EVOO
3–4 large cloves garlic
2 jalapeños
3–4 red peppers
1 large onion
1 cup chopped tomatoes

Wash, dry, salt, and pepper chicken breasts. Brown in oil with cloves of garlic and jalapeños, peeled and seeded. Add red peppers, cut in wedges and placed in pan around chicken.

In another pan, sauté large onion until golden. Add chopped tomatoes. Mix and serve over rice.

VIRGINIA'S CHICKEN CHILI

1 chicken, boned and cut up (or same amount of thighs)
¼ cup olive oil
2 onions, chopped
1 green pepper, chopped
1 small jalapeño pepper, seeded and minced
2 cans chicken broth
¼ Tbsp. cornstarch to mix with broth
1 large can chopped tomatoes
2 Tbsp. (or a little less) red wine or balsamic vinegar
1 can red kidney beans and liquid
2 cans pinto beans and liquid

Put oil in a deep pan. Add chopped onions, green pepper, and jalapeño. Sauté until vegetables are soft. Add chicken. Add broth, tomatoes, and wine or vinegar. Simmer until the chicken is cooked. Add beans and liquid

Serve with grated cheese, chopped avocado, or crumbled chips on top.

Note: Virginia buys a roasted chicken if she can. Cuts down on the cooking time.

SPICY ROASTED CHICKEN THIGHS

8 chicken thighs, with skin
5 cloves garlic, peeled
1 2-inch piece of fresh ginger root, peeled
1 small jalapeño pepper, seeded
Cayenne
Juice and zest of one whole lemon
2 tsp. tomato paste
Salt
1 tsp. cumin powder
1 tsp. coriander, either ground or seeds

Preheat oven to 425 degrees.

Pierce chicken with a small knife. Put chicken in a bowl. Mince garlic, ginger, and jalapeño. Toss with all remaining ingredients, or put into a food processor and pulse into a paste. Rub mix into chicken. Cover and refrigerate up to 24 hours if necessary.

Place chicken skin side up in a roasting pan and cook 25–30 minutes or until done.

CUT-UP LEMON ROAST CHICKEN FOR 4

1 small chicken, cut into pieces
1 head unpeeled garlic, broken into cloves
1 lemon, cut into quarters
1 small handful fresh thyme
1 Tbsp. olive oil
2/3 cup white wine
Black pepper

Preheat oven to 300 degrees.

Mix ingredients and place seasoned chicken in baking dish. Cook 2 hours.

BUTTERMILK ROAST CHICKEN

1 4-lb chicken
2 cups buttermilk
2 cloves garlic, lightly crushed
¼ cup plus 2 tablespoons vegetable oil
1 tsp. crushed black peppercorns
1 tsp. sea salt
2 tsp. fresh rosemary leaves, chopped
1 Tbsp. honey

Place chicken in large Ziploc® bag. Add buttermilk, garlic, ¼ cup oil, peppercorns, salt, rosemary, and honey. Refrigerate overnight or up to 2 days.

Preheat oven to 400 degrees.

Remove chicken from marinade and place in foil-lined pan. Drizzle with 2 Tbsp. oil. Roast for 45 minutes, then lower oven temperature to 325 degrees and roast for another 20 minutes, or until chicken is browned and the juices run clear.

MELANIE'S KING RANCH CHICKEN CASSEROLE

Recipe serves 8–10.

    20 thighs (skins on)
    2 cans chicken broth
    2 onions, chopped small
    2 stalks celery, cut into small pieces
    2–3 pods garlic, chopped
    1 pkg. corn tortillas
    Red, yellow, and green peppers
    Garlic powder
    Chili powder
    1 can cream of mushroom soup
    1 can cream of chicken soup
    Shredded cheese— Longhorn, cheddar, or Monterey Jack
    1 can Rotel® tomatoes and chilies

Boil thighs in chicken broth along with 1 onion, celery, and garlic. Shred chicken. Soften tortillas in the stock.

Preheat oven to 325 degrees.

Layer tortillas on bottom of a 9x12 glass dish. Then add layer of chicken. Add layer of remaining diced onions, along with red, yellow, and green diced peppers. Sprinkle with garlic and chili powder to taste.

Over the layered dish, spread ½ can cream of mushroom soup and 1 can cream of chicken, mixed together. Add layer of shredded cheese. Repeat layers until all ingredients used up. Sprinkle tomatoes and chilies on top.

Bake until hot.

PEGGY CLUTE'S CHICKEN

Recipe serves 10–12.

    4 2-½ lb. chickens, quartered
    1 head garlic, peeled and pureed
    ¼ cup dried oregano
    Coarse salt
    Fresh ground pepper
    ½ cup red wine vinegar
    ½ cup olive oil
    1 cup pitted prunes
    ½ cup pitted green olives
    ½ cup capers with juice
    6 bay leaves
    1 cup brown sugar
    1 cup white wine
    ¼ cup Italian parsley or cilantro, finely chopped

Combine all ingredients except sugar and wine. Marinate chicken in mix overnight.

Preheat oven to 350 degrees.

Place chicken in baking pan. Cover with marinade. Sprinkle brown sugar and divide white wine. Bake 50 minutes to 1 hour, basting often. Put on platter, baste with juice. Serve remaining juice on the side.

LEMON & GREEN OLIVE CHICKEN

Recipe serves 4.

    4 leg-thighs or 8 thighs
    2 cups white wine
    1 cup pitted green olives
    ½ cup broken walnut pieces
    1 lemon, seeded and thinly sliced
    ¼ cup coarsely chopped parsley for garnish

Preheat oven to 425 degrees.

Bake chicken for 20 minutes. Add wine and olives and cook for additional 10–15 minutes. Top with walnuts and lemon slices and cook 3 minutes. Garnish with parsley and serve.

WHOLE LEMON ROAST CHICKEN FOR 4

    1 4- to 5-lb chicken
    1 large yellow onion, sliced
    EVOO
    4 lemons—2 cut in quarters, 2 cut in wedges
    2 whole heads garlic, unpeeled and cut in half crossways
    2 Tbsp. unsalted butter
    Sea salt, ground
    Pepper, ground
    Preheat oven to 425 degrees.

Toss onion with a little olive oil and place in roasting pan. Dry whole chicken off; sprinkle cavity with salt and pepper. Place 1 head of cut garlic and 2 lemon quarters in cavity. Pat outside of chicken. Spread with melted butter and salt and pepper. Tie legs together and tuck wingtips underneath body. Place remaining garlic and lemon wedges in pan.

Roast for 1 ¼ to 1 ½ hours.

MOROCCAN CHICKEN THIGHS FOR 4

2 Tbsp. EVOO
1 lb. boneless thighs, cut into bite-sized pieces
½ cup chopped cilantro
½ cup Calimyrna figs
¼ cup chopped green olives
1 tsp. minced garlic
3 Tbsp. sweet Marsala or Madeira wine
2 Tbsp. honey
2 Tbsp. balsamic vinegar
½ tsp. ground coriander
½ tsp. ground cumin
¼ tsp. ground cardamom

Cook chicken 5 minutes in oil or until browned, stirring frequently. Stir in cilantro and remaining ingredients. Reduce heat to medium and cook 8 minutes, stirring occasionally.

FORTY CLOVE CHICKEN

Recipe serves 4.

8 chicken legs and thighs, at room temperature
and liberally salted and peppered
2 Tbsp. EVOO
1 Tbsp. unsalted butter
Lemons, cut into quarters
40 cloves garlic, peeled
½ cup dry white wine
½ cup chicken stock

Preheat oven to 375 degrees.

Place chicken pieces in a shallow baking pan, skin side up. Sprinkle oil and butter all over chicken. Cut lemon rind into pieces and place around chicken. Bury garlic beneath chicken. Cover with foil and bake for 20 minutes. Add wine and stock. Remove top and bake 15 more minutes.

JALAPEÑO CHICKEN FOR 10–12

2 cups chopped onions
2 Tbsp. butter
1 large pkg. frozen chopped spinach, cooked and drained
6 jalapeños, seeded and chopped
1 pint sour cream
3 cans cream of chicken soup
4 green onions, tops chopped off
½ tsp. salt
4–6 cups chopped cooked chicken
2 cups shredded Monterey Jack cheese

Preheat oven to 350 degrees.

Sauté onions in butter. Blend with spinach, jalapeños, sour cream, soup, onion tops, and salt. In a large pan, alternate layers of chicken, spinach mixture, and cheese, ending with cheese.

Bake for 30–40 minutes.

ROSETTA'S POLLO ALLA CACCIATORA FOR 6

(Hunter's Chicken)

12 pieces thighs and drumsticks
2 slices pancetta, cubed
EVOO
4 cloves garlic, chopped fine
1 cup white wine
1 large can tomatoes
1 tsp. rosemary
1 tsp. sage
16 mushrooms, sliced

Brown pancetta in a little olive oil. Add chicken, and cook until brown. Add garlic and sauté, then add wine and tomatoes. Simmer, adding herbs and sliced mushrooms. Simmer until cooked, about 1 and ½ hours or 1 hour and 40 minutes. Check seasonings.

If tomatoes are too watery, add 1–2 Tbsp. tomato paste.

FRIED CHICKEN FOR 4

3 lb. chicken, cut into 8 pieces
¼ tsp. salt
¼ tsp. pepper
¼ tsp. granulated onion
¼ tsp. garlic
1 egg
1 cup milk
4 cups flour
Soybean oil, enough to fill halfway up cast iron skillet

Mix seasonings into a rub. Spread over all pieces of chicken and cover. Leave chicken in fridge for a minimum of 8 hours (up to 24 hours).

Beat egg into milk in bowl. Measure out flour in separate bowl. Add 5 pinches of the seasoning mix to the flour. Dip each piece of chicken into egg/milk mixture, then coat with flour.

Heat oil in skillet to 425 degrees, or until chicken sizzles when dipped in. Put in dark meat first. Turn constantly until golden brown, about 15 minutes. Drain on paper sack for 3 minutes.

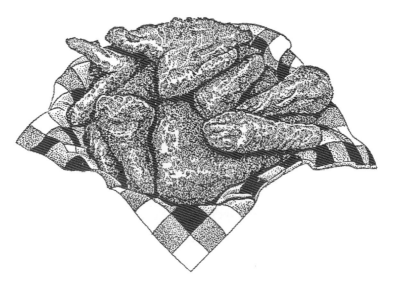

BAKED CHICKEN THIGHS WITH GINGER, THYME & YOGURT

Recipe serves 6.

    12 chicken thighs, skinned and trimmed
    2 large shallots (or 6 small)
    6 tsp. fresh ginger, minced
    ¼ cup lemon juice
    2 Tbsp. lemon zest
    1 3/4 cups plain yogurt
    2 tsp. fresh thyme leaves
    1 ½ tsp. salt

Place chicken in a baking dish large enough to line them in a single layer.

Purée remaining ingredients. Pour mixture over thighs, turning pieces to coat them on all sides. Marinate in the fridge for an hour.

Preheat oven to 425 degrees.

Bake uncovered for 55 minutes. May be served hot or cold.

CHICKEN MEDITERRANEAN

8–10 pieces of chicken, dark meat
2 Tbsp. oil
MARINADE:
2 cups lemon juice
¼ cup oil
Several cloves garlic, lightly pressed
1 quartered onion

Mix ingredients of marinate, then place in a Ziploc® bag. Marinate chicken overnight in fridge.

Preheat oven to 400 degrees.

Place drained chicken in roasting pan and drizzle with 2 Tbsp. oil. Roast for 45 minutes, then reduce heat to 325 and roast for another 20 minutes.

TUSCAN CHICKEN

2 ¼ lbs. chicken; dark meat is moister
2 ¼ Tbsp. olive oil
½ onion, sliced thin
2 cloves garlic, chopped
1 cup chicken broth
2 Tbsp. white wine
6 oz. jar artichoke hearts, drained

Sauté onions and garlic in oil. Add chicken, cooking until brown. Add broth and let simmer until the juices of the chicken are clear. Add artichoke hearts, simmer until heated, then serve.

Note: Add pitted olives for added flavor.

ANDREA'S CHICKEN ENCHILADA CASSEROLE

Recipe serves 8.

> 1 whole chicken, cooked and boned
> OR
> 4 whole chicken breasts, shredded
> 2 pkg. corn tortillas
> 1 large container of sour cream
> 1 lb. grated Monterey Jack cheese
> 1 small onion, chopped
> 3 cans green chili sauce Herdez®
> 1 Tbsp. cooking oil
> Chopped green onion tops

Preheat oven to 350 degrees.

In a 9x13 glass baking dish, place 6 tortillas on bottom. Spread sour cream over the tortillas. Sprinkle chicken over sour cream. Sprinkle with cheese and chopped onion. Pour 3/4 can of green chili sauce on top.

Repeat process, ending up with tortillas on top layer covered with sour cream, cheese, then sprinkle with chopped green onion tops.

Bake uncovered for 20 minutes.

NOTE ON HANDLING FRESH CHILI PEPPERS

The "heat" of the chili is in its seeds and veins. To work with fresh chili it is advisable to coat your fingers with a little oil to protect the skin.

IDA'S TURKEY, BEEF, OR PORK PECADILLO

2 Tbsp. EVOO
1 cup chopped red onion
1 tsp. chopped garlic
½ cup chopped red and green bell peppers
6 Tbsp. lime juice
1 lb. ground turkey (or beef or pork)
1 cup chopped tomatoes
½ cup sliced green olives
Salt and pepper
Tabasco® sauce

Heat oil in skillet. Add onion, garlic, bell peppers, and lime juice; add turkey and cook until turkey is gray. Add chopped tomatoes and green olives. Simmer 15–20 minutes to reduce liquids, but leave it juicy enough to pour over cooked rice. Season to taste with salt, pepper, and Tabasco® sauce. Garnish with chopped avocados. Good filling for soft tacos.

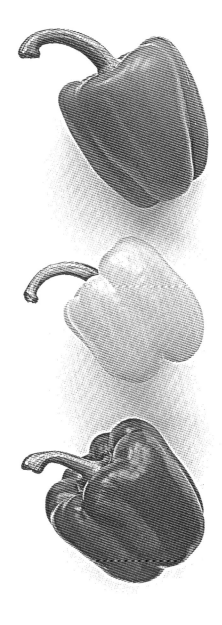

PEGGY'S VEAL

Veal
Salt
Pepper
Wondra® flour for dredging
Mushrooms
Wine
Dijon mustard
Lemon, sliced
Parsley

The above ingredients depend on the slices of veal you use.

Preheat oven to 250 degrees. Dry veal, then salt and pepper to taste. Dredge in a little Wondra®. Sauté quickly, then remove and place on oven-proof platter. Place in oven to warm. Sauté mushrooms. Deglaze pan with wine, Dijon mustard, lemon slices, and parsley. Pour over veal and serve.

ROASTED VEAL OR PORK CHOPS WITH RED GRAPES

1 lb. seedless red grapes
3 Tbsp. sherry vinegar
2 ½ Tbsp. unsalted butter, softened
½ tsp. sugar
4 1-inch thick veal rib chops, ½ lb each

Preheat oven to 500 degrees.

Toss grapes with vinegar and 1 ½ Tbsp. butter. Place in pan and roast for about 10 minutes, rolling after 5 minutes.

Rub chops with remaining butter, then season. Push grapes to one side. Add chops. Roast 5 minutes on one side, flip and roast 5 minutes on other side.

VEAL STROGANOFF FOR 6

2 to 2 ½ lbs. thinly sliced veal
¼ cup flour
1 ½ tsp. salt
¼ tsp. pepper
¼ tsp. marjoram
¼ cup cooking oil
1 cup beef broth
1 Tbsp. catsup
1 Tbsp. German mustard
1 Tbsp. Worcestershire sauce
1 cup German white wine
¼ lb. mushrooms, sliced
1 Tbsp. flour
¼ cup cold water
2 cups sour cream
2 tsp. finely chopped parsley

Cut veal into 2-inch long strips, 1 inch wide. Combine flour, salt, pepper, and marjoram. Toss meat in mixture, coating all sides. Brown in oil.

Mix broth, catsup, mustard, and Worcestershire sauce in separate bowl. Add to pan and simmer uncovered for 30 minutes. Stir in wine and mushrooms. Cook uncovered 15 minutes or until meat is tender.

Combine flour with water to make a paste. Carefully stir into skillet. Cook and stir 5 minutes. Remove from heat. Stir in sour cream. Sprinkle with parsley.

Serve over buttered noodles or spaetzle.

ROASTED MARROW BONES FOR 4

8–12 center cut beef or veal marrow bones, 3 inches long (3–4 lbs. total)
1 cup roughly chopped fresh parsley
2 shallots, thinly sliced
2 Tbsp. capers
Coarse sea salt
1 ½ Tbsp. EVOO
2 Tbsp. fresh lemon juice
Crusty bread

Preheat oven to 450 degrees.

Put bones, cut side up, on foil-lined baking pan. Cook until soft so that meat is separating from the bone but is not runny, about 15 minutes.

Combine rest of ingredients in a bowl. Whisk together.

To serve: Scoop marrow, sprinkle with salt, and top with parsley salad.

MARY FAYE'S PASTA PUTANESCA FOR 12 (WHORE'S PASTA WITH CONSIDERATIONS)

Sauce:
2 whole heads garlic, diced
2–3 Tbsp. EVOO
2 large cans diced tomatoes
3–4 cups pitted black or Calim-
era olives
1 can crushed tomatoes
3 jars capers
3–4 cups fresh mushrooms,
quartered
1 small red pepper, chopped
3 cans anchovies
2 lbs. cooked spaghetti

Sauté garlic in enough oil to make a paste.
Add diced tomatoes, chopped olives,
crushed tomatoes, capers, mushrooms, and
red pepper lightly sautéed in oil.

Note: This recipe does not require salt.

ANNE R'S PASTA BOLOGNESE

4 Tbsp. butter
½ cup finely chopped onion
1/3 cup finely chopped carrots
1/3 cup finely chopped celery
½ lb. ground veal
½ lb. ground beef
½ lb. ground pork
1 cup white wine
1 cup milk
Salt
Pepper
2 cans (28 oz) plum tomatoes with juice
½ cup heavy cream

Melt butter in wide saucepan. When foam subsides, add vegetables. Sauté and stir until tender, about 10 minutes. Add crumbled meats. Cook over low heat until meat is barely cooked through, but not browned.

Add wine and stir until wine is reduced by half. Add milk and stir over low heat for 10 minutes. Season with salt and pepper.

Puree tomatoes through a food mill into the saucepan. Cook over very low heat, occasionally stirring, for about 2 hours. Maintain a very gentle simmer. Sauce should not be allowed to boil. Taste, then salt and pepper if necessary.

Stir heavy cream into sauce. Stir until it heats through, then serve over pasta.

THIN BARBEQUED PORK CHOPS

Any number of pork chops, sliced ¼-inch thin
1 bottle Kraft's® BBQ sauce
1 onion, chopped

Trim as much extra fat off of pork chops as possible. Marinate chops in barbeque sauce with onions.

Place on barbeque. Cook 3–5 minutes on one side. Flip and cook 3–5 min on other side.

BAKED PORK CHOPS

4 pork chops
½ cup catsup
1 tsp. salt
1 tsp. celery seed
½ tsp. nutmeg
1/3 cup vinegar
1 cup water
1 bay leaf

Preheat oven to 325 degrees.

Brown chops in a skillet. Place in baking dish. Mix remaining ingredients in separate bowl, then pour over chops.

Bake for 1 hour.

PORK CHOPS WITH RED & GREEN PEPPERS

4 center-cut chops, about ½ lb. each
1 tsp. Lawry's® Seasoned Salt
1 tsp. garlic pepper
1 Tbsp. olive oil
2 tsp. chopped garlic
1 cup coarsely chopped onion
1 large red bell pepper, chopped
1 large green bell pepper, chopped
1 Tbsp. Worcestershire sauce

Brown seasoned chops on both sides in ½ olive oil over low heat until cooked through. Add remaining olive oil, garlic, and onion. Cook until translucent.

Add peppers and Worcestershire sauce. Cook until peppers are tender.

Place chops on plate and spoon peppers and onion mix over meat.

PORK CHOPS & RICE

1 cup raw rice
3 cups chicken broth
4 pretty thick pork chops
4 thick slices onion
4 lemon slices
4 dollops of catsup

Preheat oven to 350 degrees.

Put rice and chicken broth in foil-lined baking dish. Place chops on top. Add onion and lemon to each; top with catsup. Tightly cover with foil and cook for 1 ½ hours.

STUFFED PORK TENDER WITH CHUTNEY FOR 6

Pork tender
Major Grey's Chutney
Salt
Pepper
Rosemary
½ cup red wine

Preheat oven to 425 degrees.

Cut a slit in each end of the tender, then shove the handle of a long wooden spoon lengthwise through the tender, making the hole as wide as your thumb. Fill the cavity with Major Grey's chutney.

Combine salt, pepper, and rosemary in a bowl, then rub it over the exterior of the tender. Put tender in a roasting pan and pour red wine over it. Bake for 20 minutes.

Lower the temperature to 325 and cook, continuing to baste with wine every 15 minutes. After 40 minutes, remove the tender to a warm platter. Let sit for 15 minutes. Add more wine to the pan to make a sauce. Slice and serve.

ANDREA'S ONE-DISH PORK TENDER

    Pork tenderloin
    Pam® cooking oil spray
    1 potato, sliced thin
    Salt and pepper
    1 onion, sliced thin
    2–3 carrots, cut into rounds

Preheat oven to 350 degrees.

If you use a flavored tender, spray bottom of a baking dish with Pam® spray. Place sliced potato on the bottom. Spray more Pam® with light sprinkling of salt and pepper. Lay onion over the potato. Sprinkle carrots over that. Add tender and bake.

After 20 minutes, lift off the tender and stir the vegetables. When tenderloin's juices run clear, remove from oven and let sit for 10 minutes.

NANA'S HAM & PORK LOAF

    1 cup milk
    2 eggs
    1 cup soft crumbled bread, 3 thin slices
    Hot dry Colman's® mustard
    Brown sugar
    Have butcher grind together:
    1 lb. fresh pork
    1 lb. smoked ham

Preheat oven to 325 degrees.

Mix meat with milk, eggs, and bread to form a loaf. Sprinkle with a mix of dried mustard and brown sugar.

Cook for 1 ½ hours, draining fat as needed.

LAMB SHANKS DELUXE

4 meaty lamb shanks
Lemon
Garlic powder
2 tsp. salt
Pepper
1 Tbsp. olive oil
1 can of beef consommé
1 can red wine
1 can water
1 medium onion, chopped
4 carrots, sliced
1 box large brown mushrooms

Rub lamb shanks with lemon and sprinkle with garlic powder. Let stand at least 10 minutes. Place all ingredients except carrots and mushrooms (optional) in a large pan, cover, and refrigerate overnight.

Heat oven to 350 degrees and place covered pan in oven; bake 1 ½ hours. Add carrots and whole mushrooms; add more wine if needed. Cook 1 to 1 ½ hours longer.

LAMB SHANKS

Lamb shanks
Carrots, peeled and cut
Onion, chopped
1 tsp. dried thyme
Several whole cloves garlic
Dry red wine
Beef consommé

Preheat oven to 400 degrees, then lower to 350. Mix all ingredients, then place in casserole dish. Put casserole dish in oven and cook for 2 hours. Add additional vegetables, based on preference.

Uncover and season to taste. Raise oven temperature to 400 degrees. Cook another 15 minutes. Adjust seasonings for taste.

TO BROIL OR BARBEQUE BUTTERFLIED LEG OF LAMB

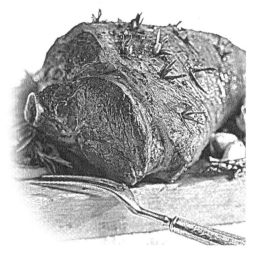

Cover both sides of leg of lamb with a paste of:

2 large cloves of garlic, puréed
½ tsp. salt
2 Tbsp. Dijon mustard
1 Tbsp. soy sauce
2 Tbsp. fresh lemon juice
1 ½ tsp. fragrant ground rosemary or
thyme or oregano (do not use combination of all three)
¼ cup EVOO

Marinate lamb for at least 1 ½ hours, or refrigerate the butterflied lamb overnight.

Cook on the barbeque or brown slowly under the broiler for 10 minutes on each side. Then let it sit at room temperature. Finish it off by roasting for 15–20 minutes on the upper rack at 375 degrees.

TACO BEEF CHILI

    1 ½ lbs. ground beef
    2 cans hominy
    2 cans pinto beans
    2 cans crushed tomatoes
    1 pkg. ranch-style powdered dressing mix
    1 pkg. powdered taco seasoning mix

Brown beef in skillet. Add cans and dressing mixes. Bring to a boil while stirring. Reduce heat and simmer 30 minutes.

Top each serving with:
    1 bag Fritos®, crushed
    Grated Longhorn cheddar
    2 chopped onions

MOTHER GILLIGAN'S POT ROAST

    1 pot roast (any variety)
    2 big onions, sliced
    Salt
    Pepper

Very important: Sear both sides of the roast until it is almost burned. This is the secret. Do not chicken out! Place cooked roast in roasting pan. Add onions, salt, and pepper. Add one inch of water. Cover tightly.

Cook pot roast at 350 degrees for 1½ hours. Time varies depending on the cut of meat. When done, remove roast. Place on platter in oven at 200 degrees.

While roast is roasting, the optional vegetables can be sautéed:
    Sliced carrots
    Mushrooms
    Onions
    Green beans

Add a side of potatoes or noodles. Put remaining gravy in a gravy boat or pitcher.

CHATEAUBRIAND (BEEF TENDER)

Preheat oven to 450 degrees.

Fold aluminum foil to make a rack. Sear roast for about 15 minutes in the oven. Lower temperature to 325 and cook roast for additional 10 minutes per pound. Let sit 15 minutes.

BEEF TENDER RARE

Tender should be at room temperature.

Preheat oven to 350 degrees.

Cook tender for 45 minutes.

DOVE OR QUAIL

Dove or quail
2 tsp. salt
2 onions, cut up
¼ cup peppercorns
Pinch or 2 paprika
2 tsp. black pepper
½ tsp. garlic salt
½ dried basil, crushed
½ tsp. dried marjoram crushed
½ cup Wondra®
Vegetable oil
2 cups red wine

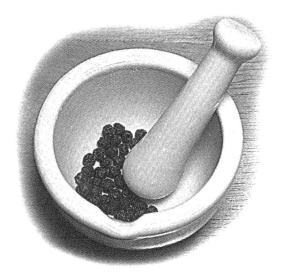

Put re-cleaned and picked over dove or quail, salt, onion, and peppercorns in water and boil for 2 hours. Let sit in broth in refrigerator.

Mix paprika, black pepper, garlic salt, basil, and marjoram into flour. Keep birds moist and dredge them in the seasoned flour.

In ½-inch of hot oil, brown birds 5 minutes on each side in a skillet. Set birds aside. Pour off grease. Add 2–4 cups liquid with ½ cup seasoned flour dissolved in it.

Cover and cook over low heat. After it begins to simmer, add red wine. Cook 45–60 minutes.

FOOLPROOF TURKEY

12 pound   2 hours; serves 8 with leftovers for sandwiches

16 pound   2 ½ hours

20 pound   3 hours

Do not truss the bird. Cover the hole with foil.

Do not pour water in the bottom of pan. Instead, use 2 Tbsp. oil to neutralize burning butter.

20 hours before cooking, swish 2 cups kosher salt into 2–3 gallons of water until dissolved. Submerge turkey in the brine using a weight to keep it underwater.

After 12 hours, rinse the bird thoroughly, pat dry, and put it in the fridge for 7 hours to completely dry the skin.

Begin stock by scoring innards and wing tips and placing into a pot. Add sliced carrot, celery stalk, large quartered onion, and a handful of parsley. Cover with stock. Simmer 3 hours, adding fluid if it gets too low or salty.

1 hour before cooking, remove turkey from fridge and bring it to room temperature.

Preheat oven to 450 degrees.

Pour 2 Tbsp. oil into bottom of pan and grease a V-shaped rack.

Stuff turkey. Rub its skin with a softened stick of butter. Place turkey on its side on the rack. Place the rack in the roasting pan and put the roasting pan in the oven.

Roast for 30 minutes. Check frequently. If turkey, juices, or pan approaches blackness, turn down heat to 400 or as low as 375.

Baste turkey. Take out the pan. Turn turkey on other side with wads of wet paper towels, or large forks placed at either end.

Set timer for 20 minutes. Baste every 20 minutes, FOUR times. Total cooking time will be 110 minutes.

Rotate turkey back to its original side, basting everything in sight.

Take turkey's temperature in the fattest point—its thigh. It should read 135 to 145 degrees. If it doesn't, leave it in for a few more minutes.

If it does, remove it immediately to the platter. Let sit for 20 minutes.

Mange!

TIME-TESTED TURKEY

Since stuffing is "outré" these days, season the cavity with salt, pepper, herbs, celery leaves, chopped carrots, and onions sautéed in butter.

Preheat oven to 325 degrees. Place prepared turkey in the lower third level. Baste with oil or accumulated juices every 30–40 minutes.

If the turkey starts to brown too much, loosely tent with foil—shiny side up.

ESTIMATED ROASTING TIMES AT 325 F:

12-16 pounds about 4 hours

16-20 pounds about 5 hours

20-26 pounds about 6 hours

Let sit for 20 minutes before carving.

BRINING A TURKEY

1 cup table salt, completely dissolved in 1 gallon water

1 cup sugar, completely dissolved in 1 gallon vegetable stock

1 tsp. peppercorns

½ tsp. spice berries

½ tsp. candied ginger

Plan to cook 10–12 hours (or 1 hour per pound)

Use a stainless steel pan or plastic bucket large enough to hold turkey.

A Reynolds® Oven-roasting bag for turkey or an extra-large Ziploc® bag can be used.

Turkey should be completely thawed and cleaned out. Do not use self basting or kosher—it's too salty. Fresh is best. Mix brine. Be sure turkey is completely covered with brine.

Keep turkey cool. Refrigerate, or if weather is cool, you can set it outside.

Rinse thoroughly before roasting.

NOTES AND VARIATIONS

MICROWAVE
HINTS

Preferred use: Glass or ceramic ovenware, glass cover, or use a plate.

Don't use plastic containers or plastic wrap.

Take slow steps. You can add more easily than you can subtract.

ARTICHOKES

Trim as usual. Put ¼ cup of water in a large measuring cup.

Flavor with garlic, lemon, and a little olive oil.

Put artichoke in upside down.

Cover cup with plate.

10 minutes on high.

ASPARAGUS

2 minutes to par boil. Cook a little longer until tender.

AVOCADOS

To ripen:

On medium (50%) for 2 minutes. Turn over and microwave 1 minute more. Or cook 30 seconds on high. This does work if the avocado is not too green. Better to microwave 30 minutes prior to peeling.

BACON

Cook on paper towel 1 minute per slice unless it's the center cut, then cook less. Be sure to cover with a paper towel to avoid spatters.

BEETS

4 minutes first pass. Check for tenderness, then microwave again.

BREAD

To warm biscuits, pancakes, or muffins that were refrigerated:

Place bread in the microwave with a cup of water. This will keep the piece moist and help reheat it faster.

CAULIFLOWER

Trim. Put in bowl with 1 Tbsp. water. Microwave about 5 minutes on high. Check before cooking further.

CITRUS FRUITS

Microwave refrigerated citrus fruits 20 seconds before squeezing.

Much juicier!

CORN

With husk on, microwave 1 ear for 4 minutes on high.

Add 2 additional minutes per ear.

Arrange multiple pieces in a triangular pattern when cooking.

EGGPLANT

Pierce with a fork and cook on high for 4 minutes.

Flip and cook 4 more minutes.

GARLIC

Roasting garlic takes 45 minutes in the oven and takes less than 8 minutes in the microwave.

Slice off the head to reveal all cloves. Place the head in a small deep dish. Season with salt and pepper. Drizzle with 2 Tbsp. olive oil. Add 2 Tbsp. water in bottom of dish. Cover tightly with plastic wrap. Cook at medium power for 7–7 ½ minutes. Let stand for a few minutes before taking off the plastic wrap.

ONIONS

Peel and wash onion. Cover with plastic wrap.

4 minutes on high.

POTATOES

Pierce an 8-oz. potato. Cook 5–7 minutes on high.

For each additional potato, add 2 ½ minutes. Be sure to pierce.

Arrange multiple potatoes in a circle when cooking.

RICE

Add 1 and ½ times as much water as rice in the serving dish you plan to use. Cover with plastic wrap with a slit in it.

12 minutes on high.

TOASTED NUTS, BREAD CRUMBS, COCONUT

Spread on plate and heat on high 2–3 minutes, stirring every minute. NOTE: They will continue to toast for about a minute after removal. Also, freshens stale nuts. 2 minutes on high.

NOTES AND VARIATIONS

AFTERS

STRAWBERRIES OR GRAPES WITH SOUR CREAM

Recipe serves 6.

1 qt. ripe strawberries or green grapes
1 pint sour cream
12 Tbsp. light brown sugar

Divide fruit into 6 dishes. Spoon 2–3 Tbsp. of sour cream over fruit in each bowl and sprinkle with 2 Tbsp. brown sugar.

PECHES AU VIN

Recipe serves 8.

6 peaches
Juice of 1 lemon
½ cup sugar
Champagne

Pour lemon/sugar mixture over peaches, sliced very thin. Refrigerate for at least 3 hours. Put in chilled champagne flutes. Cover with champagne.

ELEGANT GRAPEFRUIT

Grapefruit
Brown sugar
Butter
Rosé

Broil grapefruit sprinkled with brown sugar and butter until heated through. Before serving, dribble a nice rosé over each half and serve immediately.

LUCY BURNAP'S GREAT DESSERT

    1 can pie filling
    1 box yellow cake mix
    1 ½ stick butter
    1 cup chopped walnuts

Preheat oven to 300 degrees.

Spray a large pan with Pam spray. Mix pie filing, cake mix, and butter. Add walnuts. Bake for 1 hr. and 15 minutes.

GERI'S BLUEBERRY CRISP

    10 cups blueberries
    1 ½ cups flour
    1 cup sugar
    1 tsp. ground cinnamon
    12 Tbsp. butter, chilled

Halve the recipe for a smaller crowd.

Preheat oven to 375 degrees.

Place blueberries in a buttered baking dish or pan. Combine flour, sugar, and cinnamon in a bowl. Blend in butter until mixture is crumbly. Sprinkle over berries.

Bake about 20 minutes

Serve with vanilla ice cream.

MARY KAY'S APPLE CRISP

Preheat oven to 350 degrees.

Butter an 8x14 glass dish. Peel and cut into pieces the size of the end of your finger:

9–10 Granny Smith apples
Sprinkle with:
White sugar
Cinnamon
Nutmeg
A squeeze of lemon
Water
Dot with butter

Cover with foil and bake for 30 minutes.

Toppings:

2 sticks butter
2 cup flour
2 cups brown sugar

Sprinkle toppings over top of apples and return to oven to brown, about 20–30 minutes.

ANNE R'S WORLD-RENOWNED APPLE-PECAN BREAD

1 3/4 cups chopped apples, cored and peeled
1 ½ cups sugar
1 ½ cups flour
1 tsp. vanilla
1 tsp. baking powder
1 stick melted butter
1 egg
1 tsp. cinnamon
½ tsp. nutmeg
½ tsp. allspice
Dash salt
½ cup chopped pecans

Preheat oven to 350 degrees.

Combine all ingredients. Bake for 45 minutes to 1 hour in buttered and floured bread pan or square 8x4 pan.

MELANIE'S FAMOUS MUD PIE

1 cup flour
1 stick butter, softened
3/4 cup pecans
2 8-oz. pkg. cream cheese, softened
1 medium container Cool Whip®
½ cup powdered sugar
2 tsp. vanilla
2 pkgs. instant chocolate fudge pudding
3 cups milk

LAYER ONE:

Mix together flour, butter, and pecans and press into the bottom of a 9x13 Pyrex dish. Bake at 325 for 10–12 minutes until light brown.

LAYER TWO:

Mix softened cream cheese, 1 cup Cool Whip®, powdered sugar, and 1 tsp. vanilla until mixture is smooth and creamy. Spread on top of the "crust."

LAYER THREE:

Mix together chocolate pudding, milk, and remaining vanilla until it begins to thicken. Pour over cream cheese layer.

LAYER FOUR:

Top with remaining Cool Whip®.

Refrigerate 3–4 hours before serving.

JEN'S DEATH BY CHOCOLATE PECAN PIE

Recipe makes 2 9-inch pies.

    1 cup sugar
    1 cup Karo® syrup
    ½ cup melted butter
    4 eggs
    1 tsp. vanilla
    1 bag milk chocolate chips (12 oz.)
    1 bag chopped pecans (8 oz.)
    2 9-inch pie crusts

Preheat oven to 350 degrees.

Mix sugar, Karo®, melted butter, eggs, and vanilla. Add chocolate chips and pecans. Pour into pie crusts. Bake for 50 minutes.

ANDREA'S BLONDE BROWNIE PIE

    1 cup sugar
    ½ cup flour
    2 eggs, beaten
    1 stick (½ cup) butter, melted
    1 rounded cup semi-sweet chocolate chips
    1 cup chopped pecans
    1 tsp. vanilla

Preheat oven to 350 degrees.

In a large bowl, combine sugar, flour, eggs, and butter. Beat for 2 minutes. Fold in evenly chocolate chips, pecans, and vanilla. Scrape mixture into an 8-inch, unbaked pie shell. Bake for 45 minutes.

Cool completely, then cut into small wedges. Serve warm or at room temperature with ice cream.

FRENCH SILK PIE

1 stick butter
3/4 cups sugar
1-oz. square unsweetened chocolate
1 tsp. vanilla
2 eggs
8-inch pie crust, cooked, or graham cracker crust
½ pint whipped cream
Roasted almonds

Cream butter and sugar. Add melted, cooled chocolate and vanilla. Beat well and add one egg at a time. Pour into pre-cooked pastry shell. Cover with whipped cream. Sprinkle with roasted almonds.

AUNT CASS' SUGAR 'N SPICE COOKIES
WITH THANKS TO MICKEY MCKEE HARGRAVE

3/4 cup butter
1 egg
1 cup sugar
¼ cup dark molasses
2 cups flour
2 tsp. baking soda
¼ tsp. salt
1 tsp. cinnamon
3/4 tsp. ground cloves
3/4 tsp. ginger

Preheat oven to 375 degrees.

In one bowl, mix butter, egg, sugar, and dark molasses. In another bowl, mix flour, baking soda, salt, cinnamon, cloves, and ginger. Then combine all ingredients and drop spoonfuls on an ungreased cookie sheet.

Bake for 8 minutes.

Note: Bottoms burn if you leave them in any longer than 8 minutes.

EVELYN COLSON'S OATMEAL COWBOY COOKIES

1 cup Crisco shortening
1 cup white sugar
1 cup brown sugar
2 eggs
2 Tbsp. water
1 tsp. vanilla
2 cups flour
1 tsp. baking soda
1 tsp. salt
½ tsp. baking powder
2 cups oatmeal
1 large pkg. chocolate or butter-scotch chips
½ cup pecans

Preheat oven to 375 degrees.

Cream shortening, sugars, eggs, water, and vanilla. Add mixed dry ingredients. Add chocolate chips and pecans.

Consistency will be very dry. Roll into small balls about the size of a quarter, and place on lightly greased cookie sheet.

Bake for 10–12 minutes.

DAINTY LEMON SQUARES

1 cup flour
½ cup butter
¼ cup powdered sugar
2 eggs, beaten
1 cup sugar
2 Tbsp. lemon juice
1 Tbsp. lemon rind

Preheat oven to 350 degrees.

Combine flour, butter, and powdered sugar; mix thoroughly. Spread mixture in a 9-inch square pan. Bake for 15 minutes.

Mix together eggs, sugar, lemon juice, and rind. Spread over first layer. Return to oven for 25 minutes. When cool, frost with lemon glaze. Cut into 2-inch squares.

LEMON GLAZE

½ cup powdered sugar
1 Tbsp. lemon juice
½ Tbsp. water

Mix and spread thinly over squares.

OATMEAL SCOTCHIES

Makes about 4 dozen cookies.

  1 ¼ cups all-purpose flour
  1 tsp. baking soda
  ½ tsp. salt
  ½ tsp. ground cinnamon
  2 sticks butter, softened
  3/4 cups granulated sugar
  3/4 cups packed brown sugar
  2 eggs
  1 Tbsp. vanilla extract
  3 cups Quaker® oats
  11-oz. pkg. Nestle® butterscotch morsels

Preheat oven to 375 degrees.

Combine flour, baking soda, salt, and cinnamon in small bowl. Beat butter, both sugars, eggs, and vanilla in another bowl. Gradually beat in flour mixture. Stir in oats and morsels. Drop rounded tablespoons of mixture onto ungreased baking sheets.

Bake for 7–8 minutes for chewy, 9–10 crisp.

NANA'S COOKIES

1 stick soft butter
1 cup sugar
2 eggs
1 cup flour
1 tsp. baking powder
½ tsp. salt
1 Tbsp. vanilla

Preheat oven to 325 degrees.

Mix ingredients and stir until smooth. Drop spoonfuls on ungreased cookie sheet.

Bake for 10–12 minutes.

KELLY'S CRANBERRY & WHITE CHOCOLATE COOKIES

3 sticks butter, softened
1 cup sugar
3/4 cup brown sugar
4 eggs
1 Tbsp. vanilla
4 cups flour
1/3 tsp. salt
½ tsp. cinnamon
½ cup quick rolled oats
3/4 tsp. baking soda
1 Tbsp. lemon juice concentrate
1 ½ lbs. white chocolate chips
8 oz. raisins

Preheat oven to 375 degrees.

Cream butter and sugars; add eggs and vanilla. Beat at low speed until mixed.

Mix dry ingredients including spices in separate bowl. Slowly fold into butter mix. Add lemon concentrate and blend well. Fold in chips and raisins. Drop tablespoons of mixture onto lightly greased cookie sheet about 3 inches apart.

Bake 15 minutes or less.

PIP'S CHOCO CHIP COOKIES

NOT LIKE ANY OTHER YOU'VE EVER HAD!

Recipe makes 4–5 dozen cookies.

    1 cup butter
    1 cup vegetable oil
    1 cup brown sugar
    1 cup white sugar
    1 cup oatmeal
    1 cup Rice Krispies® (secret ingredient)
    1 cup chopped nuts
    2 cups chocolate chips
    3 ½ cups flour
    1 tsp. baking soda
    1 tsp. cream of tartar
    ½ tsp. salt

Preheat oven to 375 degrees.

Cream butter, oil, brown sugar, and white sugar. Then add remaining ingredients.
Spoon balls of mixture onto ungreased cooking sheet.

Bake 12–15 minutes.

Note: Do not substitute Rice Krispies® or cream of tartar.

ANOTHER TIME-TESTED COOKIE RECIPE

Recipe makes 112 cookies.
  2 cups butter
  2 cups brown sugar
  2 cups sugar
  4 eggs
  2 tsp. vanilla
  4 cups flour
  5 cups oatmeal (blended in blender to a fine powder)
  1 tsp. salt
  2 tsp. baking powder
  2 tsp. soda
  24 oz. chocolate chips
  1 8-oz. Hershey® bar, grated
  3 cups chopped nuts (your choice)

Preheat oven to 375 degrees.

Cream butter and both sugars. Add eggs and vanilla. Mix together with flour, oatmeal, salt, baking powder, and soda. Add chocolate chips, grated Hershey® bar, and nuts. Roll into balls. Place 2 inches apart on a cookie sheet.

Bake 10 minutes.

JACKIE PELHAM'S LONE STAR FIVE-MINUTE FUDGE

Recipe makes approximately 32 servings.

    1 12-oz. pkg. semi-sweet chocolate chips
    1 12-oz. jar smooth low-fat peanut butter
    1 14-oz. can low-fat Eagle Brand® condensed milk
    1 2-oz. pkg. chopped pecans

In a 1 ½ quart, bowl melt chocolate and peanut butter in the microwave for 3 minutes on high. Stir well to mix the two. Add the condensed milk and pecans.

Stir until mixed. Don't dawdle. This sets fast.

Pour into a wax paper-lined 8-inch pan (can use saran plastic wrap).

Refrigerate. Cut into 1-inch squares.

Each 1-inch square is 153 calories.

MELANIE'S FAMOUS RUSSIAN TEA CAKES

Recipe makes 4 dozen.

    ½ lb. butter
    ½ cup sifted powdered sugar
    2 cups sifted cake flour
    1 cup chopped pecans
    1 tsp. vanilla

Preheat oven to 325 degrees.

Cream butter; add sugar. Stir well and add flour, nuts, and vanilla. Shape into balls.

Bake on an ungreased cookie sheet for 20 minutes or until light brown. Roll in additional powdered sugar while still warm.

PHILLY'S 3-STEP WHITE CHOCOLATE CHEESECAKE

Recipe serves 8.

> 2 8-oz. pkg. Philadelphia Cream Cheese®, softened
> ½ cup sugar
> ½ tsp. vanilla
> 2 eggs
> 4 squares white baking chocolate, chopped and divided
> OR
> 2/3 cups white chocolate chips, divided
> 1 ready-to-use chocolate flavored crumb crust (6 oz. or 9 inches)

Preheat oven to 350 degrees.

Mix cheese, sugar, and vanilla with electric mixer until well-blended.

Add eggs, and mix in until blended. Stir in 1/3 cup of the white chocolate.

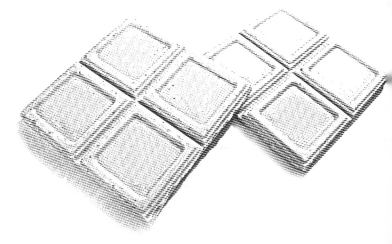

Pour into crust. Sprinkle with remaining white chocolate.

Bake for 35 minutes.

Cool. Refrigerate for 3 hours or overnight.

CROISSANT BREAD PUDDING FOR 12

6 large croissants
4 egg yolks
2 eggs
2 ¼ cups sugar
1 ½ tsp. vanilla
1 ½ tsp. salt
3 cups whipping cream
1 ½ cups light cream

Preheat oven to 325 degrees.

Tear croissants into bite-sized pieces and put in bottom of a 9x13 pan.

Combine remaining ingredients in a bowl and whisk until thoroughly mixed. Pour mixture over croissants. The tops should show.

Place pan in a larger pan filled with one inch warm or hot water; water should come up around outside of 9x13 pan.

Bake 45 minutes or until a knife inserted in the center comes out clean.

Remove from water bath and cool.

NOTES AND VARIATIONS

COCKTAILS

STOCKING THE BAR

How much wine and liquor will you need for a party?

At a dinner party, each adult will probably drink three glasses of wine. Some resources say 2 ½ glasses per person—adjust accordingly.

If you are serving two wines, allow one glass of the appetizer wine and 1 ½ of the entrée wine.

At a party, a good guideline is one drink per adult each half hour. This means all beverages, including soft drinks, juices, mineral water, and alcohol.

Remember, more people are drinking red these days.

A regular bottle of wine or champagne holds four 6-oz. glasses. Therefore, a case will provide 48–50 glasses.

BRANDY FREEZE

> ½ gallon coffee ice cream
> 1 ½ oz. Crème de Cocoa
> 1 ½ oz. Drambuie
> 1 ½ oz. Cointreau
> 8 oz. brandy

Put half of the ice cream in a blender. Combine liqueurs and add half the mixture. Blend well. Add the second halves and blend again. Store in the freezer until ready to serve.

BOURBON MILK PUNCH

1 gallon vanilla ice cream
1 cup bourbon
1 cup rum
¼ cup brandy
Freshly grated nutmeg

Place softened ice cream in a punch bowl. Add bourbon, rum, and brandy.

Stir well until blended. Sprinkle with nutmeg.

BLOODY MARY

1 oz. vodka
2 oz. tomato juice
1 dash lemon juice
2 dashes salt
2 dashes black pepper
2 dashes cayenne
3 dashes Worcestershire sauce

Mix all but vodka. Pour vodka over ice. Add mix. Stir. Then serve.

OLD-FASHIONED EGGNOG

12 eggs, separated
1 cup sugar
1 quart milk
2 cups bourbon
1 cup rum
1 quart whipping cream

Beat egg yolks, adding sugar a little at a time. Pour in milk, bourbon, and rum. Chill several hours. Beat egg whites until stiff. Fold into egg mix. Fold in whipped cream. Sprinkle with freshly grated nutmeg to taste.

MARGARITA

8 oz. Minute Maid® limeade
8 oz. tequila
1 oz. triple sec
1–2 scoops ice

Mix and serve.

MARGARITA FOR 2

1 6-oz. can frozen limeade
Juice of 2 limes
3 oz. triple sec
6 oz. tequila

Mix and serve.

TEQUILLA SOUR

1 can Minute Maid® lime juice
Juice of 6 limes
10 ice cubes, crushed
1 ½ cans tequila

Mix and serve.

SANGRIA FOR 6

½ orange, peeled and seeded
2 cups diced strawberries or peaches
Zest of ½ lemon
2 tsp. granulated sugar
1 cup Valpolicella or port
1 bottle of dry white wine, well-chilled

Slice orange into thin wedges. Toss fresh fruit with other ingredients with the port. Allow the fruit to macerate about an hour.

Pour mix into a carafe and fill with cold white wine.

SANGRIA FOR 2

1 bottle red wine
1 small bottle of soda
1 ½ cup brandy
1 ½ oz. Cointreau or Triple Sec
3 tsp. sugar
Lemons and oranges, sliced

Toss fresh fruit with other ingredients. Chill and serve.

GOOD ROSÉ WINES

Chateau Routas "Rouviere"

Sola Rosa Rosé, California

E. Guigal Tavel

Domaine Tempier Bandol Rosé

M. Chapoutier Coreaux du Tricastin

Bodegas Ochoa Garnacha Navarra Rosado

NOTES AND VARIATIONS

TRILLIUM
TIPS

SEVEN WAYS TO LOSE "FALSE FAT"

Cut out wheat, bread, pasta, and cereal. Wheat is one of the top seven allergens.

Eliminate dairy. Eliminate sugar. Try a fruit and vegetable fast for three days. See above. Don't drink. Alcohol is a form of super-sugar.

Try counting calories. Most people think if they eat the "right food" they can eat all they want.

Try the old switcheroo. If you've been on high protein, switch to vegan.

BASIC FAT BURNING SOUP

8 carrots
2 cans green beans*
1 large onion, chopped coarse
2 cans tomatoes*
1 large head of cabbage
2 green peppers
1 bunch celery, chopped
1 pkg. Lipton® onion soup mix
1 cup beef broth
2–3 cloves of garlic (optional)

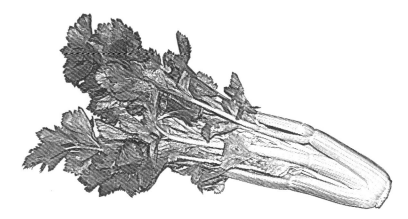

Cut up vegetables in large, bite-sized pieces, cover with water, and boil fast for 10 minutes. Cut to simmer and continue cooking until vegetables are crunchy. Season with saltless garlic salt and ground pepper.

* I used Furmano's® Romano cut green beans and Furmano's® Italian style diced tomatoes. Put in with rest of the ingredients. Real tasty.

Note: This soup may be eaten any time you are hungry. Eat as much as you want, any time you want. The more you eat, the more you lose. You can expect a 5–7 lb weight loss after 7 days. Just remember, when you start eating again … back comes the weight!

ONE-WEEK DIET

DAY ONE: Fruits. Cantaloupe, honeydew, and other melons are cheaper in calories. NO BANANAS.

DAY TWO: Vegetables. All you can eat. Lots of leafy greens. No corn or legumes or fruit.

DAY THREE: Fruits. Vegetables.

DAY FOUR: 3 bananas and skimmed milk. 1 banana each meal. Lots of water. Soup.

DAY FIVE: Beef and tomatoes. 15–20 oz. meat and as many as 6 fresh tomatoes. 6–8 glasses of water. At least 1 soup.

DAY SIX: Beef or skinless chicken and veggies. 2 or 3 steaks with green leafy vegetables. At least 1 soup.

DAY SEVEN: Brown rice, unsweetened fruit juice, and veggies. At least 1 soup.

DEFINITE NO-NOS: NO ALCOHOL, BREAD, SODAS, DIET DRINKS. NO FRIED FOODS.

GAYLORD HAUSER'S CLEANSING BROTH

1 cup finely shredded celery (leaves and all)
1 cup finely shredded carrots
½ cup shredded spinach
1 tsp. shredded parsley
1 qt. water
1 cup tomato juice
1 tsp. vegetable salt
Pinch of brown sugar or honey

Put all the shredded vegetables into 1 qt water. Cover and cook slowly for 25 minutes. Add tomato juice, vegetable salt, and pinch of sweetener. Cook a few more minutes. Strain and serve.

VANILLA TIPS

FYI: Vanilla beans are the fruit of an orchid—the only orchid known to bear edible fruit.

2 teaspoons vanilla to 1 gallon latex paint eliminates the odor.

To deodorize the refrigerator, put a few drops vanilla on a cotton ball. Place on a saucer.

To deodorize a stinky cooler, wash the inside of the cooler with ¾ cup bleach to 1 gallon of hot water. Then saturate a cloth with vanilla and wipe down the inside.

DID YOU EVER THINK OF?

- To get more juice out of fresh lemons, bring them to room temperature and roll them under your palm on the kitchen counter before cutting.

- Burnt food in a skillet? Put a little dish soap in it, cover with water, bring to boil.

- Before you pour a sticky substance into a measuring cup, fill it with hot water. Dump out the water but don't dry the cup. Next add your ingredient like peanut butter and watch how easily it comes out.

- When a cake recipe calls for flouring the pan, use a little of the cake mix.

- If you over-salt a dish, drop in a peeled potato to absorb the extra salt.

- To reheat pizza, use a nonstick skillet on top of the stove. Use medium-low heat, and heat until warm. Keeps the crust crispy.

- To reheat refrigerated biscuits, pancakes, and muffins: Place them in the microwave with a cup of water. The increased moisture will keep the food moist and help it reheat faster.

- To expand frosting (a container of cake frosting bought at the store), whip it with your mixer for a few minutes. It will double in size.

- Wrap celery in aluminum foil before refrigerating. It will keep for weeks.

- Store opened chunks of cheese in aluminum foil. It will stay fresh much longer and will not develop mold.

- Hardened brown sugar? Put a slice of apple in the box or microwave for 15–30 seconds to soften.

- Bananas: Peel from the bottom. No more little stringy things. Separate your bananas after you buy. This slows down the ripening process.

- Cure for headaches? Take a lime, cut it in half, and rub it on your forehead. (Or, better still, put lime in a rum toddy, and after a few of those, you won't know the difference!)

- Don't throw out that leftover wine. Freeze into ice cubes for cooking.

- A raw potato will take the food stains off your fingers. Rinse.

- Garlic or onion odor on your fingers? Rub fingers on the stainless part of a kitchen knife under water.

- Peppers with 3 bumps on the bottom are sweeter and better for using raw. Peppers with 4 bumps are firmer and better for cooking.

- Add a teaspoon of water when frying ground beef. It will help pull the grease away from the meat while cooking.

- To make scrambled eggs or omelets really rich, add a couple spoonfuls of sour cream, cream cheese, or heavy cream and then whip.

- Add garlic immediately to a recipe if you want a light taste and at the end of a recipe if you prefer a stronger taste.

- To get rid of the itch from a mosquito bite, apply soap.

- To get rid of ants: Use chalk. Draw a line on the floor. They won't cross it.

- Put small piles of cornmeal where you see the ants. They can't digest it. May take a week or so but it does work.

- Good-bye fruit flies! Fill half a small glass with cider vinegar and add 2 drops of dishwashing liquid. It does the trick.

- For a splinter: Cover it with Scotch® tape and pull off tape.

- A spritz of hairspray will drive bees and flies away.

- BUT if the bee stings, use a meat tenderizer or WD-40®.

- Sunburn? Empty a large jar of Nestea® into your bath water.

- Burn your tongue? Put sugar on it.

- To reopen a sealed envelope: Put envelope in the freezer for a few hours, then slide a knife under the flap. The envelope can then be resealed.

- To reduce static cling, pin a small safety pin in the seam of your skirt or seam of your slacks.

- Use an empty toilet paper roll to store appliance cords. You can write what appliance it belongs to on the roll.

- To get something out of a heat register or from under a refrigerator, attach an empty gift wrap or a paper towel roll to the end of a vacuum.

- Crayon marks on walls? A damp rag dipped in baking soda and a little elbow grease. Or apply toothpaste and brush it.

- Dirty grout? Listerine®.

- Permanent marker on appliances or counter tops? Rubbing alcohol on a paper towel.

- Broken glass: Use a wet cotton ball or a Q-tips® swab to pick up the small shards you can't see easily.

- Cut SOS® pads in half. Also, sponges with SOS®-type material on back do great in quarters.

- Bloodstains on clothes? Pour a little peroxide on a cloth and wipe.

- Fungus on toenails or fingernails? Apply Vicks VapoRub®

- Put candles in the freezer 3 hours before using. They laaast!

- Fresh Flowers? Add a little bleach, or 2 aspirin, or simply use 7-Up® instead of water.

- Peanut butter can remove labels off glassware and take scratches out of CDs.

- Any cola will take the grease stains off the driveway overnight, the gunk off battery terminals, and rust out of toilet bowls.

- Bread is delivered fresh to the store 5 days a week—every day EXCEPT Wednesday and Saturday.

- The twists or plastic tags are:

- Blue – Monday

- Green – Tuesday

- Red – Thursday,

- White – Friday

- Yellow – Saturday.

- They are also used alphabetically: B, G, R, W, Y. Easy to remember.

THINGS GO BETTER WITH BOUNCE®

CAUTION: Using any type of dryer sheet will eventually "clog" the dryer's lint filter. Test-run water through the filter. If it pools on top, gently wash the filter with soapy water and a scrub brush.

- If the filter is not kept free of this build-up, the dryer motor can burn out or worse still, catch on fire. Other than this caveat, go for it!

- Chases ants. Put sheet nearby.

- Repels mosquitoes, bees, and yellow jackets. Tie a sheet through belt loop when outside.

- Repels mice. Spread sheets around. Also good in stored cars.

- Eliminate static electricity from your television and computer screens.

- Dissolves soap scum from shower doors.

- Run a needle through a sheet to prevent thread from tangling.

- Put a sheet in a dirty pot or pan. Fill with water. Let sit overnight.

- Wipe Venetian blinds. Prevents dust from resettling.

- Wipe over flyaway hair. Collect loose cat, dog, or human hairs.

- In the bag of a vacuum cleaner.

- Takes odor out of books and picture albums that aren't used often.

- Bottom of a waste basket, especially in the kitchen.

- In empty luggage before storing.

- Deodorize shoes or sneakers.

- Storing sleeping bags.

TWO OR MORE TABLETS OF ALKA SELTZER® CAN:

- Clean a toilet (wait 20 minutes, brush, then flush).

- Remove stains from bottom of a deep vase or cruet.

- Polish jewelry (2 minutes).

- Clean a thermos bottle. This takes FOUR tablets and an hour or more.

- Unclog a drain. THREE tablets followed by a cup of white vinegar.

PAM® IS MORE THAN A COOKING SPRAY

- A spritz will dry finger nail polish.

- Free up a sticking bicycle chain.

- Remove paint and grease from skin.

CLUB SODA

- Soak to clean jewelry and gem stones.

- Use on a fresh carpet spill. Let soak a few and sponge up.

- Takes the green "chlorine" out of blond hair.

- Loosens rusty nuts and bolts.

- Gentle scrubbing with club soda is an easy way to get greasy stains out of double-knit fabrics.

- Sponge club soda into any food stain, then wash item as usual.

WD-40®—A MIRACLE!

- Protects silver from tarnishing.

- Removes road tar and grime from cars.

- Cleans and lubricates guitar strings.

- Gets oil spots off concrete driveways.

- Gives floors that "just-waxed" look without making them slippery.

- Cleans and restores chalkboards.

- Removes lipstick stains—saturate and wash.

- Untangles jewelry chains.

- Removes stains from stainless steel sinks.

- Removes dirt and grime from barbeque grill.

- Keeps ceramic/terracotta garden pots from oxidizing.

- Removes tomato stains from clothing.

- Keeps glass/plastic shower doors free of water spots.

- Camouflages scratches in ceramic/marble floors.

- Keeps scissors working smoothly.

- Lubricates noisy door hinges in home and cars.

- Rids rocking chairs of squeaks.

- Lubricates tracks in sticking windows.

- Makes umbrella stems easier to open and close.

- Lubricates fan belts on washers and dryers.

- Keeps rust from forming on tools.

- Removes spattered grease on stove.

- Keeps bathroom mirror from fogging.

- Keeps pigeons off the balcony (they hate the smell).

- Removes all traces of duct tape or any adhesive.

- Removes and cleans insects from grills.

- Spray a LITTLE on live bait and wait for the BIGGEST FISH.

- Takes the sting out of fire ant bites.

- Removes crayon from walls.

- Removes black scuff marks from flooring.

STAINS

CRANBERRY SAUCE AND OTHER BERRIES:

WASHABLES: Flush the area with cold water. Use an eyedropper to apply a solution of one part white vinegar and two parts water. Let sit 10 minutes. Next apply SHOUT® or ZOUT® and finish with a regular wash cycle.

NON-WASHABLES: Blot with cold water. Use an eyedropper to apply the vinegar solution. Follow with an application detergent such as WOOLITE® and water to clean the residue.

SALAD DRESSING:

WASHABLES: Shake on talcum powder or cornstarch to soak up as much oil as possible. Pick or scrape off the excess, then let dry. Apply a combination solvent such as SHOUT® and let sit for fifteen minutes. Finish with a regular cycle.

NONWASHABLES: Shake on talcum powder or cornstarch to soak up as much oil as possible. Pick or scrape off the excess, then let dry. Apply an oil solvent such as CARBONA STAIN DEVIL #5® (www.carbona.com) for store locations). Let dry, then scrape or brush off any remaining stain.

CHOCOLATE:

WASHABLES: Treat the spot with a solution made from a tablespoon of an enzyme detergent such as WISK® and two cups of water. Let stand for 20 minutes then rinse thoroughly.

NONWASHABLES: Apply rubbing alcohol, let sit for 10 minutes, then rinse carefully. Use a combination of water and a mild detergent such as WOOLITE® to clean the residue.

WAX:

WASHABLES: Let wax harden, or freeze by placing it in the freezer for 20 minutes. Scrape off as much as possible. Stretch the fabric over a bowl, then from a height of about one foot, carefully pour boiling water over spot to clean the residue.

NONWASHABLES: Let wax harden, or freeze by placing it in the freezer for 20 minutes. Scrape off as much as possible. Apply an oil solvent such as CARBONA STAIN DEVIL #5® to clean residue.

COFFEE:

WASHABLES: Use an eyedropper to apply a solution of one part white vinegar and two parts water, THEN RINSE. If the coffee had milk or sugar in it, follow with an enzyme detergent like WISK® and water. Let sit for 10 minutes. Finish with a regular wash cycle.

NONWASHABLES: Apply a gentle detergent like WOOLITE® and water. Rub to form suds, then rinse. Next, use an eyedropper to apply a solution of one part white vinegar and two parts water, then rinse. If the coffee had milk or sugar in it, finish by applying an oil solvent such as CARBONA STAIN DEVIL #5® and let dry.

www.louisegaylord.com